FIELD GUIDE

Creatures Great and Small

Illustrated by

Lucy Engelman

How to use this book

CHOOSE A PRINT

There are 35 prints in this book, all featuring wonderful animals from around the world. Beautiful fish, spectacular birds, incredible insects, and remarkable mammals are vying for your attention. So what are you waiting for? Pick a print and get started.

COLOR IT IN

On the back of each print, you'll find interesting facts about each of the species featured on the front, including what colors they are. However, don't feel like you have to be true to life. Get creative with your colored pencils or crayons. Have fun!

PULL IT OUT AND FRAME IT!

You can easily pull each print out of the book. When you have done so, you'll have a beautiful piece of art —personalized by you—to hang on your wall or give to a friend.

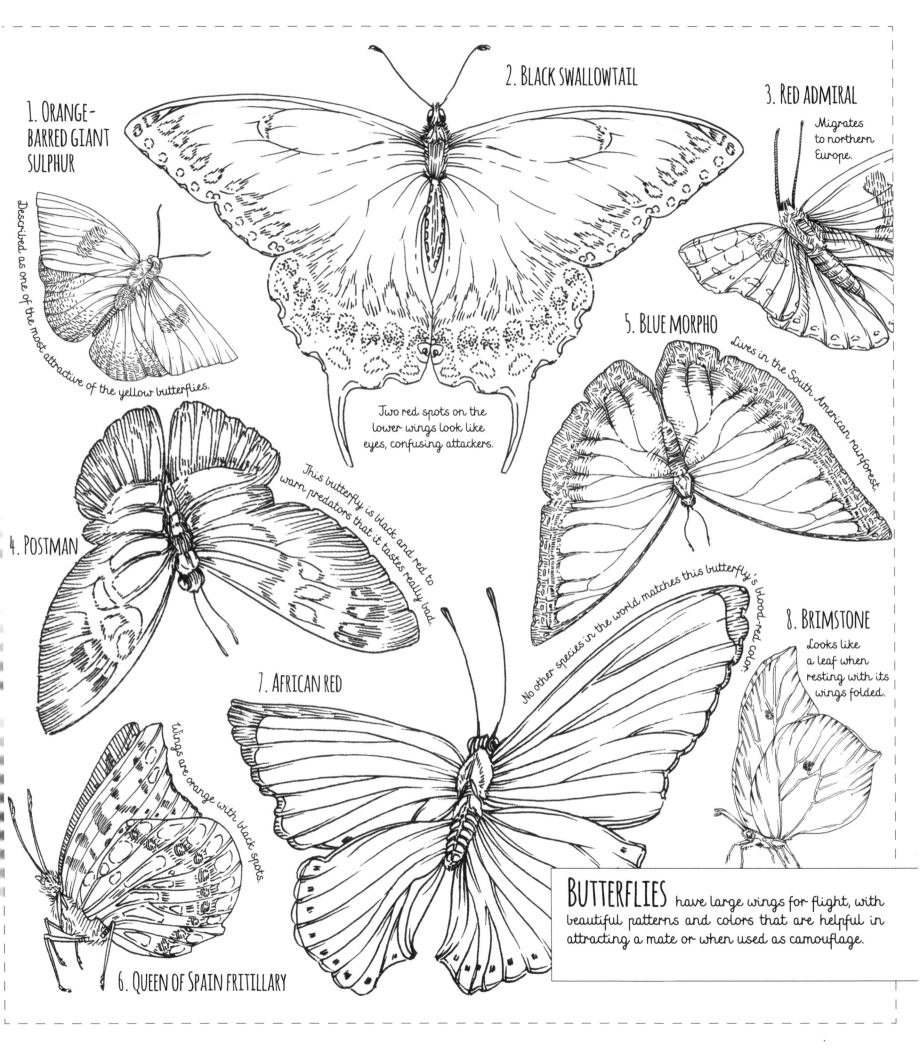

1. ORANGE-BARRED GIANT SULPHUR

Described as one of the most attractive of the yellow butterflies.

2. BLACK SWALLOWTAIL

Two red spots on the lower wings look like eyes, confusing attackers.

3. RED ADMIRAL

Migrates to northern Europe.

4. POSTMAN

This butterfly is black and red to warn predators that it tastes really bad.

5. BLUE MORPHO

Lives in the South American rainforest.

No other species in the world matches this butterfly's blood-red color.

6. QUEEN OF SPAIN FRITILLARY

Wings are orange with black spots.

7. AFRICAN RED

8. BRIMSTONE

Looks like a leaf when resting with its wings folded.

BUTTERFLIES have large wings for flight, with beautiful patterns and colors that are helpful in attracting a mate or when used as camouflage.

KEY

1. ORANGE-BARRED GIANT SULPHUR

With its three-inch wingspan and vibrant yellow-and-orange coloring, this has been described as one of the most attractive of the yellow butterflies. It is found at the edge of subtropical forests.

2. BLACK SWALLOWTAIL

The black swallowtail has black wings with lines of yellow and blue dots on the edges. To confuse predators, it has two red spots on its lower wings. Its false eyes draw attention away from its soft body parts.

3. RED ADMIRAL

Originating from Africa, the red admiral migrates to northern Europe. Some migrate south again but many stay, only to be killed by the northern winter climate. They are brown with red and white markings.

4. POSTMAN

Postman butterflies are brightly colored to warn predators that they taste unpleasant. Their slender black and red wings have white edges. They eat the pollen and suck the nectar of passion-fruit flowers.

5. BLUE MORPHO

This iridescent blue butterfly lives in the South American rainforest. The underneaths of its wings are brown, which blends in against trees, so when it flies as it beats its wings it seems to appear and disappear.

6. QUEEN OF SPAIN FRITILLARY

The Queen of Spain fritillary is a strong, fast-flying butterfly. It can migrate over long distances, flying over two thousand feet high while searching for food. Its wings are orange with black spots.

7. AFRICAN RED

No other species of butterfly in the world has the blood-red color of the African red. Its wings are edged in black. This relatively small butterfly is found in forested areas in Central Africa.

8. BRIMSTONE

To blend in with its surroundings, the underside of the male brimstone butterfly is a yellowish-green color, so that when resting with its wings folded up, it looks like a leaf. Each upper wing is yellow with an orange spot.

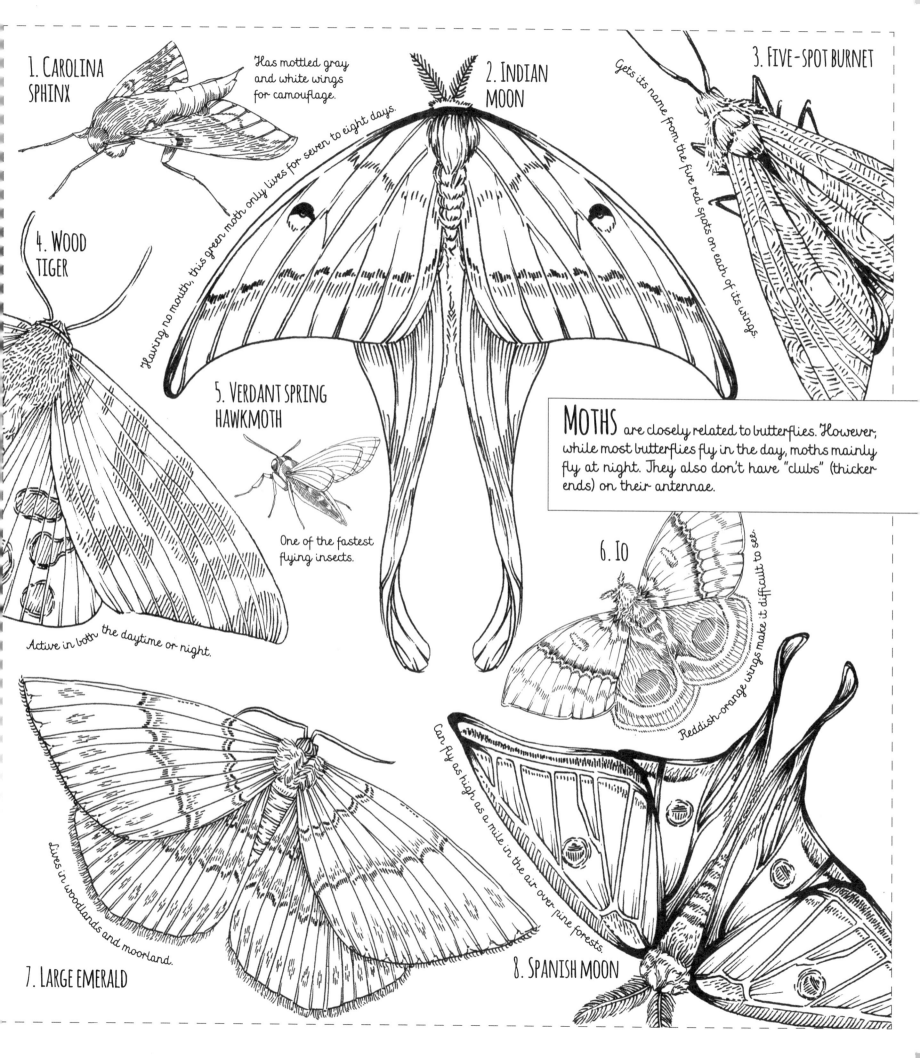

1. CAROLINA SPHINX

Has mottled gray and white wings for camouflage.

2. INDIAN MOON

Having no mouth, this green moth only lives for seven to eight days.

3. FIVE-SPOT BURNET

Gets its name from the five red spots on each of its wings.

4. WOOD TIGER

Active in both the daytime or night.

5. VERDANT SPRING HAWKMOTH

One of the fastest flying insects.

MOTHS are closely related to butterflies. However, while most butterflies fly in the day, moths mainly fly at night. They also don't have "clubs" (thicker ends) on their antennae.

6. IO

Reddish-orange wings make it difficult to see.

7. LARGE EMERALD

lives in woodlands and moorland.

8. SPANISH MOON

Can fly as high as a mile in the air over pine forests.

KEY

1. CAROLINA SPHINX ....

When threatened, the Carolina sphinx moth shows the bright colors on its abdomen to startle the attacker. Its mottled gray and white wings provide camouflage when this moth rests on tree bark or on rocks.

2. INDIAN MOON ....

The pale green Indian moon moth has no mouth parts, meaning it cannot feed, and so lives for only seven to eight days, just long enough to mate and lay eggs. Males can detect the scent of a female three miles away.

3. FIVE-SPOT BURNET ....

This moth gets its name from the five red spots on each of its black wings, which warn birds that it isn't pleasant to eat. The lower wings are bright red. The five-spot burnet moth prefers to fly in bright sunlight.

4. WOOD TIGER ....

Found in habitats such as woodland clearings, heaths, and moors as far as Japan, the wood tiger moth can be active in both the daytime or night. Its upper wings are black with yellow lines. Its lower wings are orange.

5. VERDANT SPRING HAWKMOTH ....

With its long, narrow wings and torpedo-shaped body, the hawkmoth is one of the fastest flying insects. Its upper wings, head, and body are green. The lower wings are made up of patches of orange, red, black, and white.

6. IO ....

The Io moth's upper wings are a reddish-orange color, which make it difficult to see. If threatened, the moth reveals two huge eye spots on its lower wings. This startles attackers, giving the moth time to fly away.

7. LARGE EMERALD ....

The large emerald moth has bright green wings—especially when newly emerged from its cocoon—which are covered in white lines. Its range extends as far north as the Arctic Circle, living in woodlands and moorland.

8. SPANISH MOON ....

This beautiful moth—which is becoming rare—can fly as high as a mile in the air over pine forests. Its wings are greenish-blue with brown lines across them, and are edged in light yellow, while its body is orange-brown.

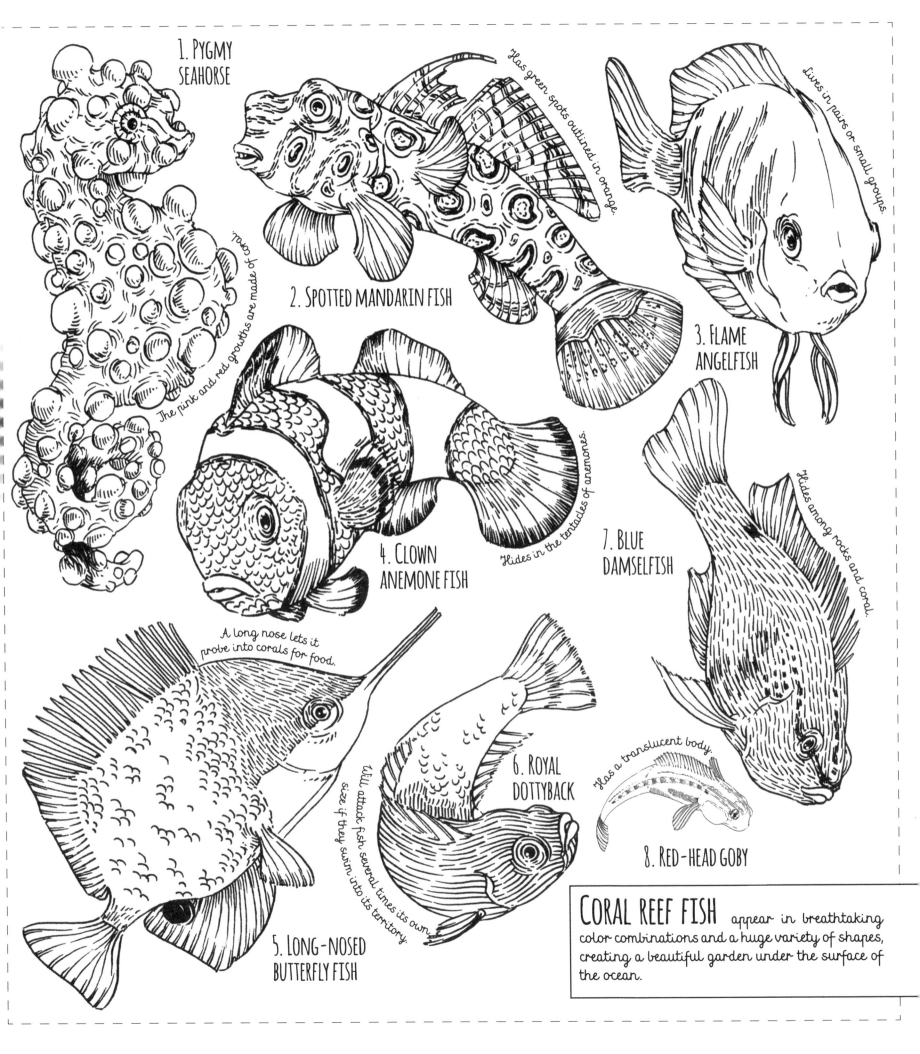

1. PYGMY SEAHORSE

The pink and red growths are made of coral.

2. SPOTTED MANDARIN FISH

Has green spots outlined in orange.

3. FLAME ANGELFISH

Lives in pairs or small groups.

4. CLOWN ANEMONE FISH

Hides in the tentacles of anemones.

7. BLUE DAMSELFISH

Hides among rocks and coral.

5. LONG-NOSED BUTTERFLY FISH

A long nose lets it probe into corals for food.

6. ROYAL DOTTYBACK

Will attack fish several times its own size if they swim into its territory.

8. RED-HEAD GOBY

Has a translucent body.

CORAL REEF FISH appear in breathtaking color combinations and a huge variety of shapes, creating a beautiful garden under the surface of the ocean.

KEY

1. PYGMY SEAHORSE

This small species of seahorse is whitish-gray with pink and red warty growths all over. These warts are actually made of coral that grows on the creature's body to give the seahorse perfect camouflage.

2. SPOTTED MANDARIN FISH

The spotted mandarin fish is bright green, with dark green spots outlined in orange and black. It might look difficult to miss, but its bright colors make it hard to spot in its natural habitat: different types of algae.

3. FLAME ANGELFISH

Flame angelfish live in pairs or small groups and graze the reef eating sponges, algae, and tiny crustaceans. Their bright red bodies have rear blue edges and an orange patch in the middle with black stripes.

4. CLOWN ANEMONE FISH

These bright orange, white-striped fish live within the tentacles of some anemones. The fish initially makes brief contact with the anemone's stinging cells, after which it can live among them without being harmed.

5. LONG-NOSED BUTTERFLY FISH

The dark area on the face of the long-nosed butterfly fish conceals its real eyes, while a false eye at the back deters attackers. The rest of the fish is bright yellow. Its long nose is ideal for probing into corals for food.

6. ROYAL DOTTYBACK

Each royal dottyback maintains a territory of several square yards and will attack fish many times its own size if they swim into its territory. The front half of its body is magenta and the rear half bright yellow.

7. BLUE DAMSELFISH

Blue damselfish live in a community which is close to a "safe" area. When danger threatens, they dart away to hide among rocks and coral. They get their name from their electric-blue coloring, but they have yellow tails.

8. RED-HEAD GOBY

Gobies are the largest family of fish that live in the sea, though some have evolved to live in freshwater habitats. This small species has a brilliant red head with gold and blue stripes, and a translucent body.

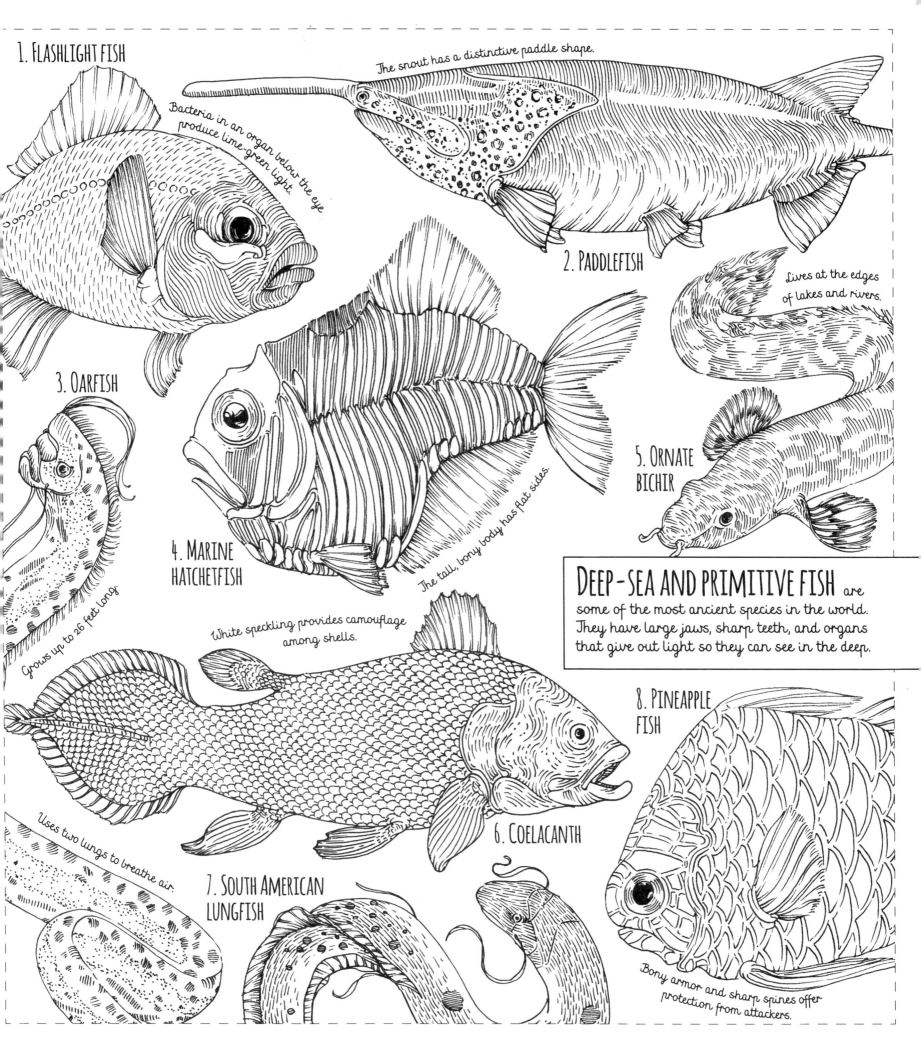

1. FLASHLIGHT FISH

Bacteria in an organ below the eye produce lime-green light.

The snout has a distinctive paddle shape.

2. PADDLEFISH

Lives at the edges of lakes and rivers.

3. OARFISH

Grows up to 26 feet long.

4. MARINE HATCHETFISH

The tall, bony body has flat sides.

5. ORNATE BICHIR

DEEP-SEA AND PRIMITIVE FISH are some of the most ancient species in the world. They have large jaws, sharp teeth, and organs that give out light so they can see in the deep.

White speckling provides camouflage among shells.

8. PINEAPPLE FISH

Uses two lungs to breathe air.

7. SOUTH AMERICAN LUNGFISH

6. COELACANTH

Bony armor and sharp spines offer protection from attackers.

KEY

1. FLASHLIGHT FISH ······················

The dark-colored flashlight fish gets its name from the lime-green light produced by bacteria living in an organ below its eye. It can turn this light on and off by using a flap of skin. Down its side are pale blue spots.

2. PADDLEFISH ·······················

Paddlefish have distinctive paddle-shaped snouts. They sweep through the sea with their mouths open, taking in lots of water which they filter to get plankton. Their skin is blueish-gray and doesn't have scales.

3. OARFISH ·······························

Growing to lengths of 26 feet, oarfish have rarely been seen alive, as they live at depths of 650 feet. Their pelvic fins end in a tip which looks like an oar. They have a silver body with dark red fins.

4. MARINE HATCHETFISH ··············

Along both sides of the silver marine hatchetfish is a row of organs which produce light. These can blink on and off to attract food and mates, while confusing predators. When they're on, the fish appears pink.

5. ORNATE BICHIR ·····················

Ornate bichirs live at the edges of lakes and rivers, and have the ability to breathe air. They are yellowish in color with a black net-like pattern. Prey is stalked, and then, when within range, sucked into the bichir's mouth.

6. COELACANTH ·······················

The coelacanth was believed to be extinct, but it was rediscovered in 1938. Its white speckling provides effective camouflage among the shells of the rocky reefs it inhabits. The rest of it is colored blue-gray.

7. SOUTH AMERICAN LUNGFISH ·······

Having small gills, the gray South American lungfish uses two lungs to breathe air. In the dry season, it survives for several months by coating itself with mucus and resting in a chamber of moist mud.

8. PINEAPPLE FISH ···················

Bony armor and sharp spines protect the pineapple fish from attackers. It gets its name from its yellow scales edged with black. Below the jaw is a light organ, so the fish can see when hunting at night.

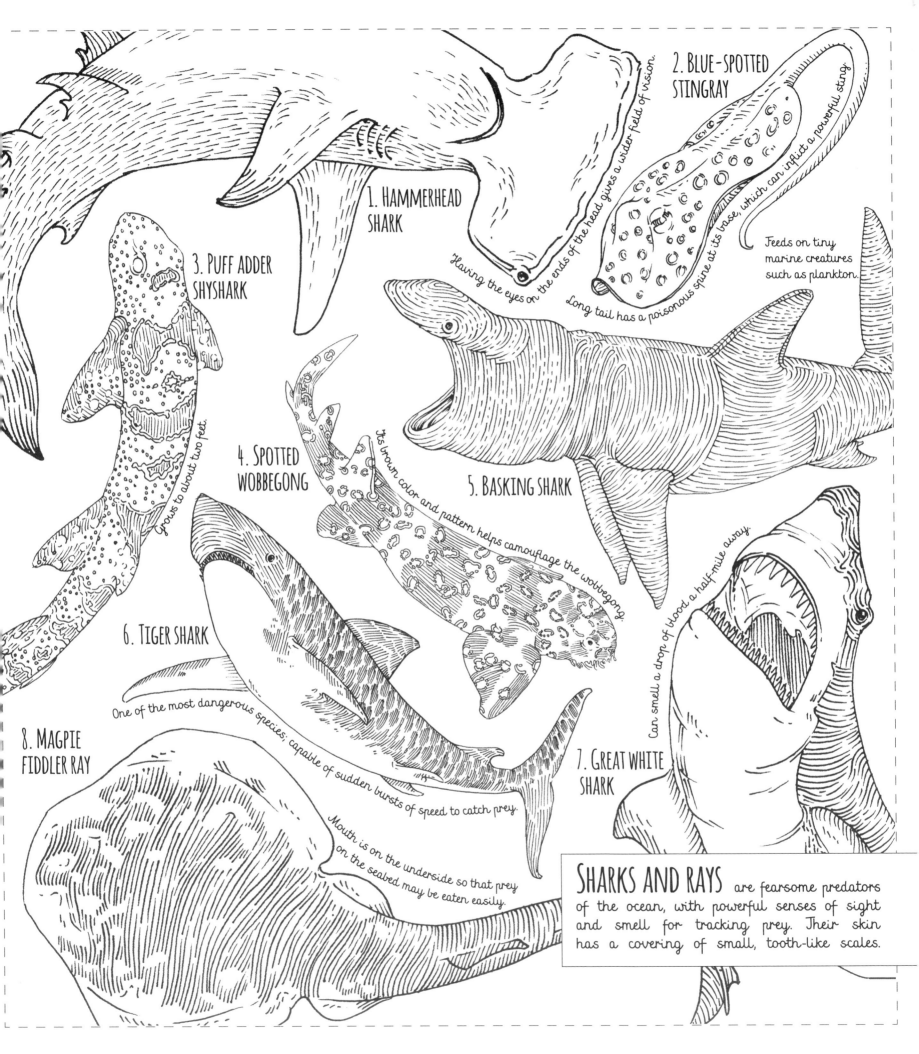

1. HAMMERHEAD SHARK

Having the eyes on the ends of the head gives a wider field of vision.

2. BLUE-SPOTTED STINGRAY

Long tail has a poisonous spine at its base, which can inflict a powerful sting.

Feeds on tiny marine creatures such as plankton.

3. PUFF ADDER SHYSHARK

Grows to about two feet.

4. SPOTTED WOBBEGONG

Its brown color and pattern helps camouflage the wobbegong.

5. BASKING SHARK

6. TIGER SHARK

One of the most dangerous species; capable of sudden bursts of speed to catch prey.

7. GREAT WHITE SHARK

Can smell a drop of blood a half-mile away.

8. MAGPIE FIDDLER RAY

Mouth is on the underside so that prey on the seabed may be eaten easily.

SHARKS AND RAYS are fearsome predators of the ocean, with powerful senses of sight and smell for tracking prey. Their skin has a covering of small, tooth-like scales.

Key

1. HAMMERHEAD SHARK

The strange shape of hammerhead sharks enables them to move better to catch prey, as having the eyes on the ends of their head gives them a wider field of vision. They are gray-brown with white undersides.

2. BLUE-SPOTTED STINGRAY

These stingrays, which are yellowish-green with blue spots, often lie buried in sand with just the eyes showing. The long tail has a poisonous spine at its base and can inflict a powerful sting if stepped on.

3. PUFF ADDER SHYSHARK

Growing to about two feet, the golden-brown, white-spotted puff adder shyshark is not dangerous to humans. It is found at depths of up to 420 feet, where it feeds on squid, worms, and shellfish.

4. SPOTTED WOBBEGONG

Wobbegongs are slow-moving, bottom-dwelling sharks. Their brown color and spotted pattern helps disguise them on the seabed, where they lie in wait to ambush passing crustaceans.

5. BASKING SHARK

Despite the basking shark's huge size—growing up to 33 feet—it is harmless, only feeding on tiny marine creatures with its huge, gaping mouth. Its body and fins are gray with pale, irregular lines.

6. TIGER SHARK

One of the most dangerous species, tiger sharks are known man-eaters. They are capable of sudden bursts of speed to catch prey. Their bodies are grayish-green and have a stripy pattern similar to the tiger cat.

7. GREAT WHITE SHARK

Great white sharks can smell a drop of blood a half-mile away and swim at a speed of 30 miles per hour, making them formidable hunters. Their undersides are white but their bodies are dark gray.

8. MAGPIE FIDDLER RAY

The rare and beautiful magpie fiddler ray is found off the coast of South Australia. Its edges and fins are yellow and its markings blueish-black. The mouth is on its underside so it can easily eat prey from the seabed.

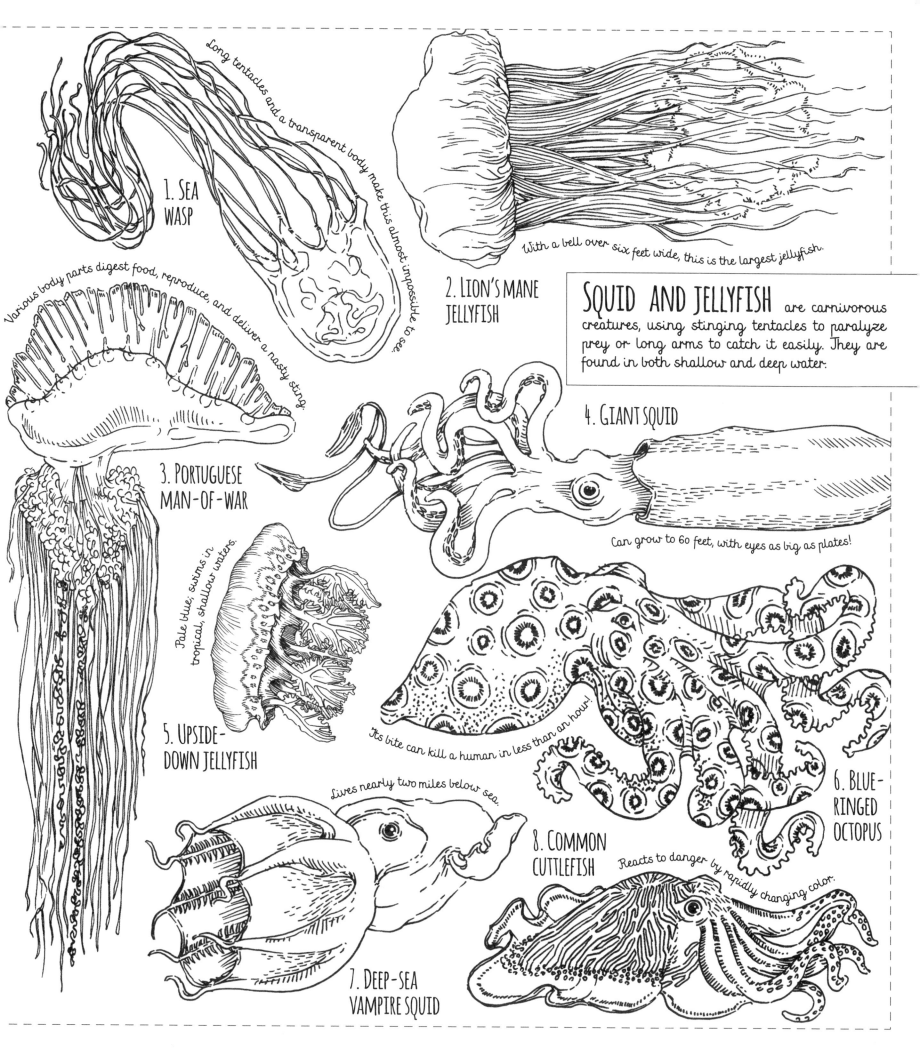

1. SEA WASP

Long tentacles and a transparent body make this almost impossible to see.

2. LION'S MANE JELLYFISH

With a bell over six feet wide, this is the largest jellyfish.

SQUID AND JELLYFISH are carnivorous creatures, using stinging tentacles to paralyze prey or long arms to catch it easily. They are found in both shallow and deep water.

Various body parts digest food, reproduce, and deliver a nasty sting.

3. PORTUGUESE MAN-OF-WAR

4. GIANT SQUID

Can grow to 60 feet, with eyes as big as plates!

Pale blue, swims in tropical, shallow waters.

5. UPSIDE-DOWN JELLYFISH

Its bite can kill a human in less than an hour!

6. BLUE-RINGED OCTOPUS

Lives nearly two miles below sea.

8. COMMON CUTTLEFISH

Reacts to danger by rapidly changing color.

7. DEEP-SEA VAMPIRE SQUID

KEY

1. SEA WASP

The sea wasp is also known as the box jellyfish because of the shape of the bell (body). The venom in its long tentacles is capable of killing a human in five minutes. It is almost transparent, but has a green tinge.

2. LION'S MANE JELLYFISH

Unlucky fish easily become paralyzed by the barbed stings in the pale blue tentacles of the lion's mane jellyfish. The bell—which grows to over six feet wide— is gray with blue or purple rings.

3. PORTUGUESE MAN-OF-WAR

The Portuguese man-of-war is made up of four parts that work together: The pink tentacles deliver a nasty sting to attackers, while another part reproduces, and another digests. The top is filled with gas, providing flotation.

4. GIANT SQUID

Growing to about 60 feet, the pale orange giant squid has eyes as big as dinner plates! It grabs prey with two 40-foot arms and eight tentacles, holding it tight with powerful gray suction cups.

5. UPSIDE-DOWN JELLYFISH

Unlike most jellyfish, the pale blue bell of the upside-down jellyfish sits below its tentacles. It lives in tropical, shallow waters attached to the sandy seabed. Pods filled with algae around its mouth give it nutrition.

6. BLUE-RINGED OCTOPUS

Despite its small size of only four inches, the blue-ringed octopus has a venomous bite which can kill a human in less than an hour. The shade of blue of its body changes according to its mood.

7. DEEP-SEA VAMPIRE SQUID

The deep-sea vampire squid lives nearly two miles below sea level, where the waters are inky-black. Its dark color blends into the background, allowing it to sneak up on prey undetected.

8. COMMON CUTTLEFISH

Common cuttlefish have orangey-pink backs, but can rapidly change color—and also squirt black ink— to confuse predators. Using eight arms and two long tentacles, they are able to catch prey easily.

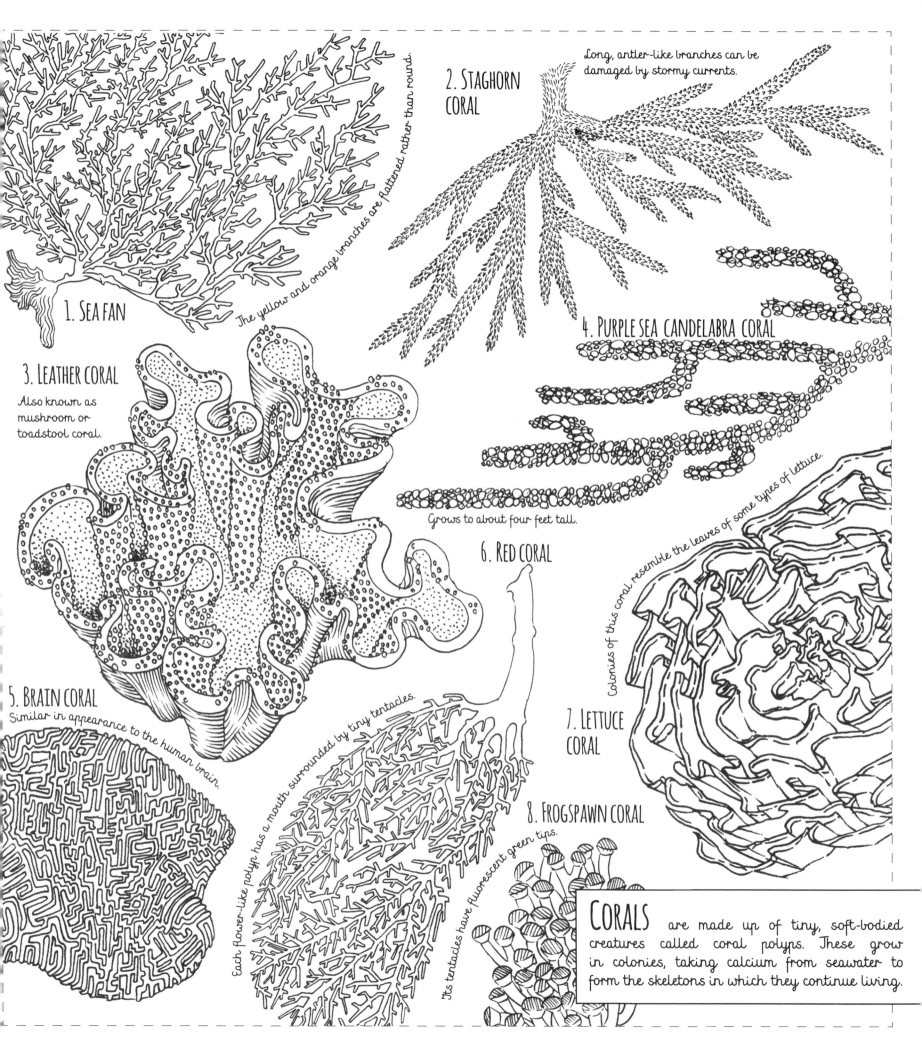

1. SEA FAN

2. STAGHORN CORAL

Long, antler-like branches can be damaged by stormy currents.

The yellow and orange branches are flattened rather than round.

3. LEATHER CORAL

Also known as mushroom or toadstool coral.

4. PURPLE SEA CANDELABRA CORAL

Grows to about four feet tall.

5. BRAIN CORAL
Similar in appearance to the human brain.

Each flower-like polyp has a mouth surrounded by tiny tentacles.

6. RED CORAL

7. LETTUCE CORAL

Colonies of this coral resemble the leaves of some types of lettuce.

8. FROGSPAWN CORAL

Its tentacles have fluorescent green tips.

CORALS are made up of tiny, soft-bodied creatures called coral polyps. These grow in colonies, taking calcium from seawater to form the skeletons in which they continue living.

Key

1. SEA FAN

The sea fan is bright yellow, becoming orange nearer the base. If the fan is knocked away from the base, which remains on the reef, it is possible for a new fan to grow. The branches are flattened rather than round.

2. STAGHORN CORAL

Staghorn coral has long, antler-like branches which grow quickly, although strong currents and stormy weather can break them. They can be found in a variety of colors including yellow and blue.

3. LEATHER CORAL

Also known as mushroom or toadstool coral, this coral has a thick base and grows upward in twists and folds. It is creamy white with fine red tentacles and brightly colored polyps (growths).

4. PURPLE SEA CANDELABRA CORAL

Purple sea candelabra coral is a soft coral, meaning it doesn't grow a stony skeleton, so when it dies, little is left behind. It grows to about four feet tall. It is purple with small white polyps.

5. BRAIN CORAL

The polyps of brain corals may grow up to an inch in diameter. They are arranged in their thousands in meandering rows that form a pattern similar to the human brain.

6. RED CORAL

Red coral is a soft, branching coral within which are many tiny, flower-like polyps. Each has a central mouth surrounded by minuscule tentacles. At night, these are extended to catch food.

7. LETTUCE CORAL

Colonies of this coral resemble the ruffled leaves of some types of lettuce, although the colors are not the same (lettuce coral is purple with blue edges). The species grows in cloudy water on the edges of reefs.

8. FROGSPAWN CORAL

Frogspawn coral has brownish-purple tentacles with fluorescent green tips. On some, the tips are hammer-shaped. The large, fleshy-looking polyps are extended during the day.

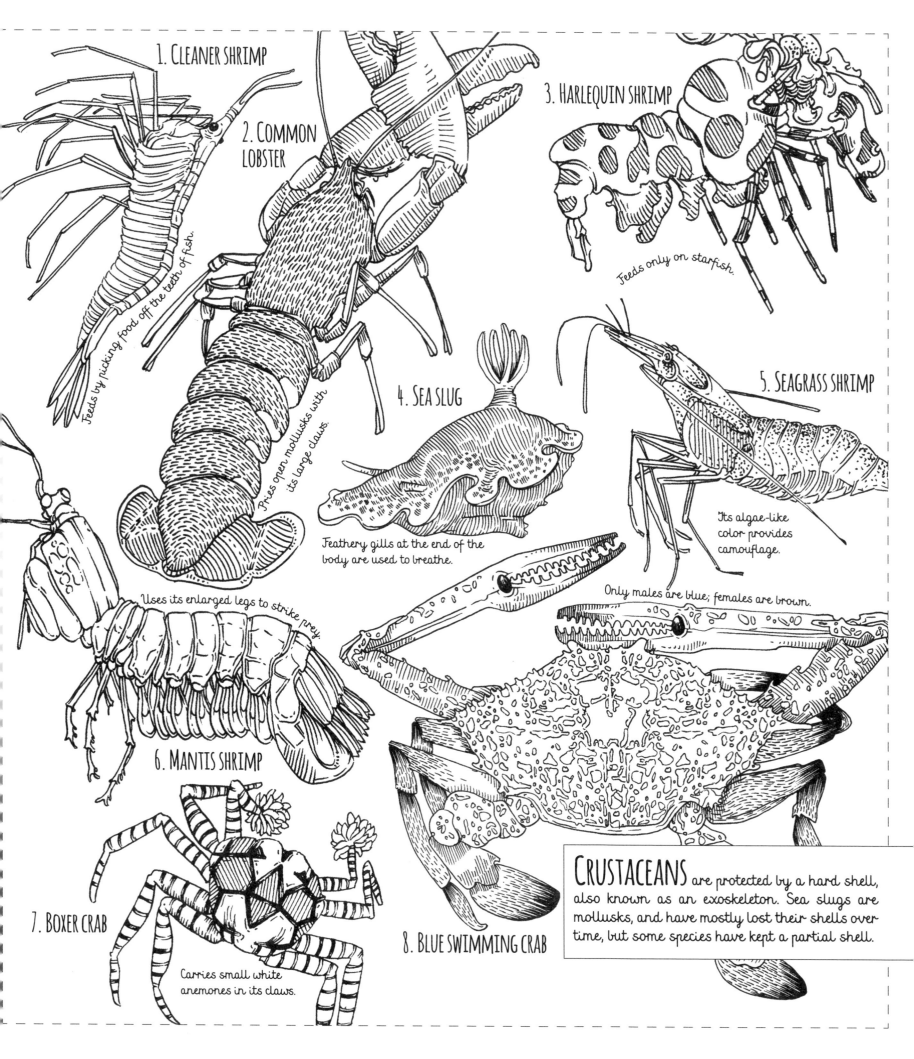

1. CLEANER SHRIMP

2. COMMON LOBSTER

3. HARLEQUIN SHRIMP

Feeds only on starfish.

Feeds by picking food off the teeth of fish.

Pries open mollusks with its large claws.

4. SEA SLUG

5. SEAGRASS SHRIMP

Its algae-like color provides camouflage.

Feathery gills at the end of the body are used to breathe.

Only males are blue; females are brown.

Uses its enlarged legs to strike prey.

6. MANTIS SHRIMP

7. BOXER CRAB

8. BLUE SWIMMING CRAB

Carries small white anemones in its claws.

CRUSTACEANS are protected by a hard shell, also known as an exoskeleton. Sea slugs are mollusks, and have mostly lost their shells over time, but some species have kept a partial shell.

Key

1. CLEANER SHRIMP ....

Fish remain still while the white-banded cleaner shrimp cleans inside their gills and mouth, picking food off the fish's teeth without fear of being bitten. The shrimp has yellow sides and a red stripe down its body.

2. COMMON LOBSTER ....

Common Lobsters frequent rocky areas, finding crevices in which to rest. They are blue with yellow undersides and blueish-gray claws, which they use to pry open mollusks and eat the soft inner parts.

3. HARLEQUIN SHRIMP ....

Colored white with brown spots ringed in blue and purple stripes on their legs, harlequin shrimp look like the harlequin orchid flower. They feed only on starfish, particularly the arms and tube feet.

4. SEA SLUG ....

This species of sea slug eats some sponges as well as algae and flatworms. The feathery external gills placed toward the rear of the body are for breathing. It is yellow-orange with purple spots.

5. SEAGRASS SHRIMP ....

The emerald-green color of the seagrass shrimp provides effective camouflage among algae and other marine plants. It can darken its color, and even take on a brownish hue if it is next to brown vegetation.

6. MANTIS SHRIMP ....

This mantis is a "smasher"—the enlarged legs are used to strike prey, including shelled creatures such as crabs. Its greenish-blue body has white lines on it, while its antennae and legs are red.

7. BOXER CRAB ....

The boxer crab's name comes from the small, white anemones it carries in its claws, which look like boxing gloves. It uses these "gloves" for defense. It is white, with pink shapes on its body and pink bands on its legs.

8. BLUE SWIMMING CRAB ....

Only male blue swimming crabs are blue; females are a dull brown. They all have very long claws that are covered in sharp teeth to catch food. When threatened, they sometimes bury themselves in the sand.

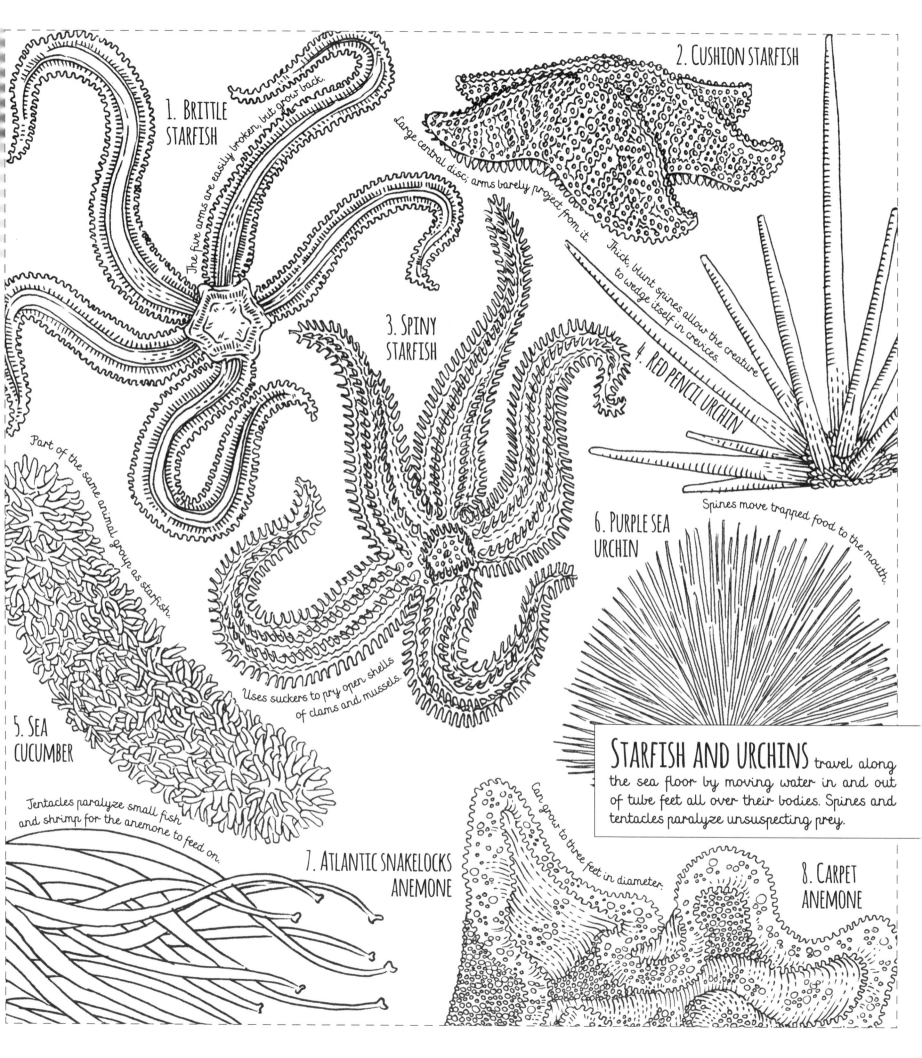

1. BRITTLE STARFISH

The five arms are easily broken, but grow back.

2. CUSHION STARFISH

Large central disc; arms barely project from it.

3. SPINY STARFISH

Uses suckers to pry open shells of clams and mussels.

4. RED PENCIL URCHIN

Thick, blunt spines allow the creature to wedge itself in crevices.

Spines move trapped food to the mouth.

5. SEA CUCUMBER

Part of the same animal group as starfish.

6. PURPLE SEA URCHIN

STARFISH AND URCHINS travel along the sea floor by moving water in and out of tube feet all over their bodies. Spines and tentacles paralyze unsuspecting prey.

7. ATLANTIC SNAKELOCKS ANEMONE

Tentacles paralyze small fish and shrimp for the anemone to feed on.

Can grow to three feet in diameter.

8. CARPET ANEMONE

Key

1. BRITTLE STARFISH ....

The five long, narrow arms of the gray-black brittle starfish are easily broken, but grow back. A scavenger, the starfish relies on two of its arms to pull itself along while looking for food.

2. CUSHION STARFISH ....

Unlike other starfish, gray cushion starfish place their eggs in a sheltered spot instead of just shedding them into the water. The central disc is large, with arms that barely project from it. They have yellowish spines.

3. SPINY STARFISH ....

To feed, spiny starfish pry open clam shells and mussels with their powerful suckers, then they extend their stomachs through their mouths to suck out the contents. They are red with yellow spines.

4. RED PENCIL URCHIN ....

Red pencil urchins have fewer spines than other urchins, but the spines they have are very thick and blunt, helping the creature wedge itself in crevices. Tiny shrimp often live in the spines.

5. SEA CUCUMBER ....

Sea cucumbers are part of the same animal group as starfish and sea urchins. They use small, tentacle-like tube feet to get around and for feeding, and come in many different colors, including orange, red, and blue.

6. PURPLE SEA URCHIN ....

The mouth on the underside of the sea urchin is made up of five plates that work like jaws. As the urchin moves slowly over rocks, its purple spines grasp algae found on the surface, then move it to the mouth.

7. ATLANTIC SNAKELOCKS ANEMONE ....

Around 180 long, stinging, green tentacles with lilac tips surround the mouth of the Atlantic snakelocks anemone. These have the job of paralyzing small fish and shrimp for the anemone to feed on.

8. CARPET ANEMONE ....

Found on shallow, flat reefs, the bright green carpet anemone can grow to three feet in diameter in warm, sunlit waters. Its carpet-like appearance comes from its many bead-like tentacles.

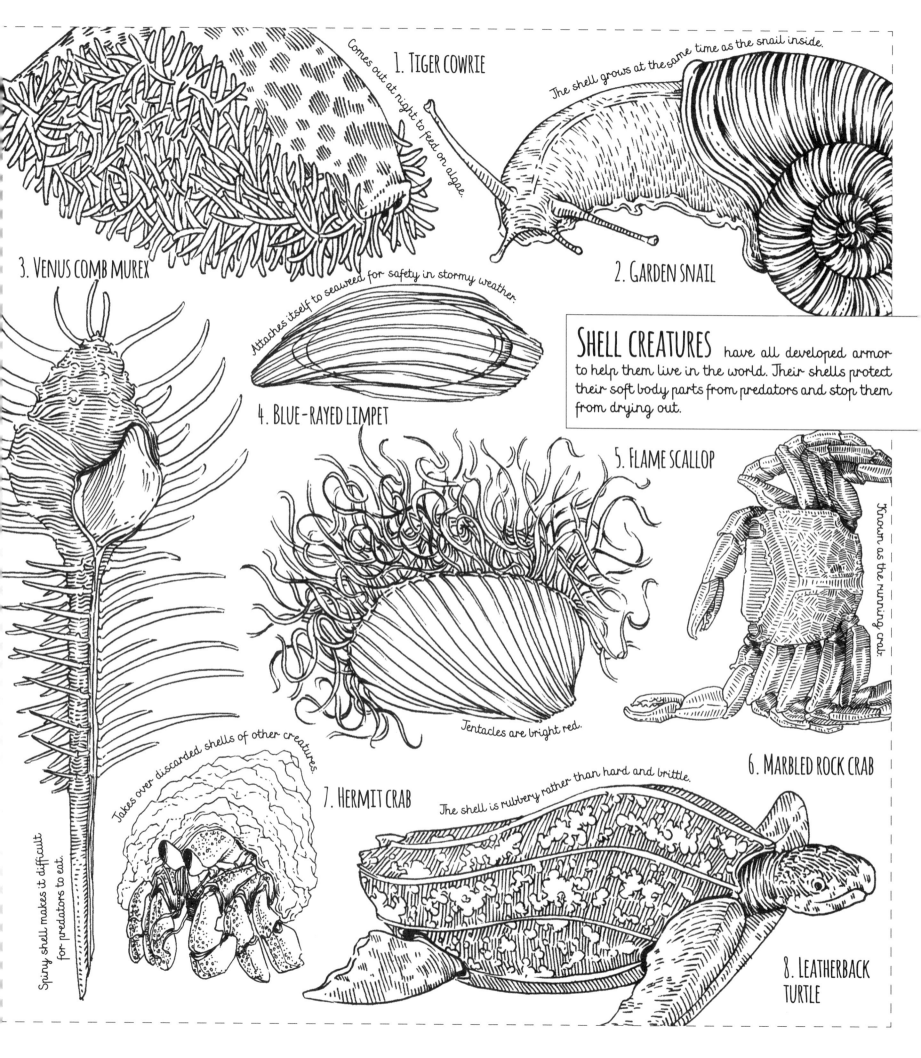

1. TIGER COWRIE

Comes out at night to feed on algae.

The shell grows at the same time as the snail inside.

2. GARDEN SNAIL

3. VENUS COMB MUREX

Attaches itself to seaweed for safety in stormy weather.

4. BLUE-RAYED LIMPET

SHELL CREATURES have all developed armor to help them live in the world. Their shells protect their soft body parts from predators and stop them from drying out.

5. FLAME SCALLOP

Known as the running crab.

Tentacles are bright red.

Takes over discarded shells of other creatures.

Spiny shell makes it difficult for predators to eat.

7. HERMIT CRAB

6. MARBLED ROCK CRAB

The shell is rubbery rather than hard and brittle.

8. LEATHERBACK TURTLE

Key

1. Tiger cowrie

Tiger cowries are nocturnal. They hide away during the day among corals or in crevices, and come out at night to feed on algae. Their shell is mottled black, light brown, orange, and cream.

2. Garden snail

A mucus gland produces a sticky slime which helps the garden snail move on its muscular foot. Its yellow-brown shell grows at the same time as the brown snail grows inside.

3. Venus comb murex

The spiny shell of the Venus comb murex makes it tough for predators to get to the entrance and eat the soft-bodied snail within. It can be cream, gray, white, or sandy in color.

4. Blue-rayed limpet

The blue-rayed limpet has a light brown shell with electric-blue streaks. By attaching itself to roots that anchor seaweed to rocks, the limpet avoids being swept away during stormy weather.

5. Flame scallop

To escape predators such as starfish, the red-tentacled flame scallop uses jet propulsion. A special muscle opens and closes the two shells, quickly expelling a stream of water, propelling itself away.

6. Marbled rock crab

The marbled rock crab is also known as the running crab due to its ability to speed over rocks and squeeze into cracks to avoid pursuers. It is bright green with darker green and brown marbling.

7. Hermit crab

The hermit crab takes over the discarded shells of other marine creatures. It needs a shell to protect its soft abdomen. As the crab grows, it looks for a slightly larger shell to move into. Its legs are blue and black.

8. Leatherback turtle

Leatherback turtles are unusual in that the shell—colored black with white markings—is rubbery rather than hard and brittle. One of its favorite foods is jellyfish, as it is immune to its stinging cells.

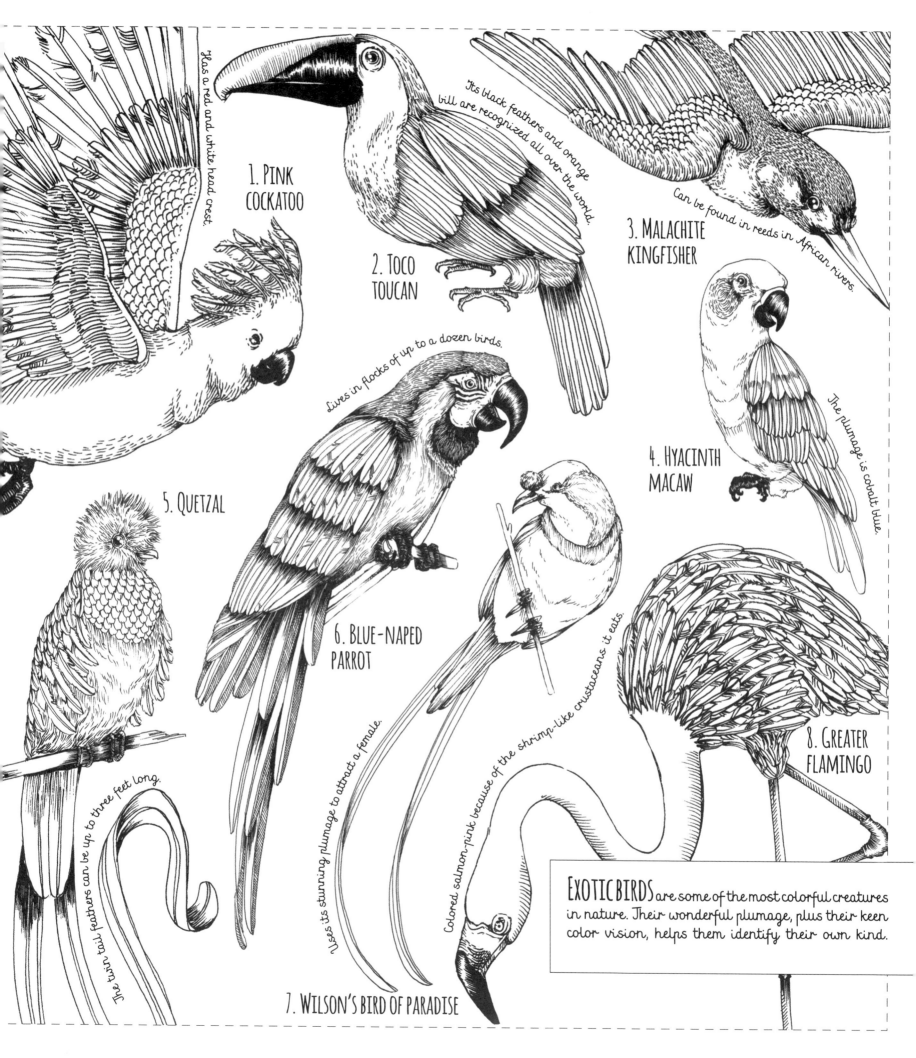

1. PINK COCKATOO

Has a red and white head crest.

2. TOCO TOUCAN

Its black feathers and orange bill are recognized all over the world.

3. MALACHITE KINGFISHER

Can be found in reeds in African rivers.

4. HYACINTH MACAW

The plumage is cobalt blue.

5. QUETZAL

The twin tail feathers can be up to three feet long.

6. BLUE-NAPED PARROT

Lives in flocks of up to a dozen birds.

7. WILSON'S BIRD OF PARADISE

Uses its stunning plumage to attract a female.

8. GREATER FLAMINGO

Colored salmon-pink because of the shrimp-like crustaceans it eats.

EXOTIC BIRDS are some of the most colorful creatures in nature. Their wonderful plumage, plus their keen color vision, helps them identify their own kind.

KEY

1. PINK COCKATOO ....

This bird, also known as Major Mitchell's cockatoo, has a white and pale-pink body with a bright red and white head crest. It lives in woodlands in areas of Australia that get little or no rain.

2. TOCO TOUCAN ....

The South American rainforest is where the Toco toucan lives, although its black feathers and bright orange bill are recognized all over the world. The bill is used to catch food—mainly fruit and insects.

3. MALACHITE KINGFISHER ....

A river bird, the Malachite kingfisher can be found in reeds in Africa, south of the Sahara. Its upper parts are bright metallic blue while its underside is orange. It uses its black and red bill to catch fish.

4. HYACINTH MACAW ....

Hyacinth macaws live in the rainforest and can be spotted flying over the canopy with their long tails streaming behind. Their plumage is cobalt blue, with yellow around the eye and at the base of their beaks.

5. QUETZAL ....

During the mating season, to attract a female, male quetzals grow twin tail feathers, which can be up to three feet long. The quetzal's plumage is a brilliant blue-green. Males have bright red chests.

6. BLUE-NAPED PARROT ....

This parrot can be found in the Philippines, where it lives in flocks of up to a dozen and feeds on mangoes, berries, seeds, nuts, and grain. Its body is bright green with a turquoise tinge to its head. Its beak is red.

7. WILSON'S BIRD OF PARADISE ....

This small bird of paradise uses its stunning blue, red, yellow, and emerald-green plumage to attract a mate. A male will select a clearing then thrust his bright chest forward and flick his long, curved tail feathers.

8. GREATER FLAMINGO ....

A diet of shrimp-like crustaceans is responsible for the flamingo's famous salmon-pink color. These tall birds favor habitats like lakes and estuaries, where they use extensive mudflats for breeding and feeding.

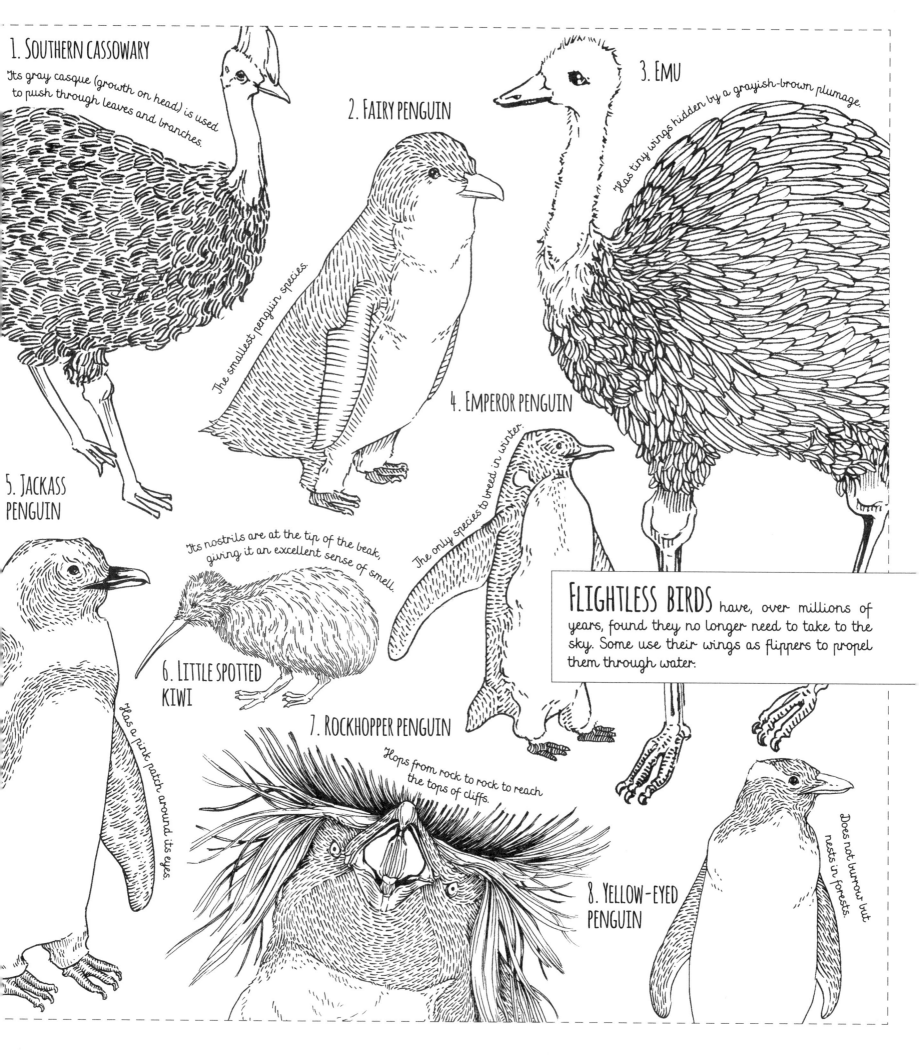

1. SOUTHERN CASSOWARY

Its gray casque (growth on head) is used to push through leaves and branches.

2. FAIRY PENGUIN

The smallest penguin species.

3. EMU

Has tiny wings hidden by a grayish-brown plumage.

4. EMPEROR PENGUIN

The only species to breed in winter.

5. JACKASS PENGUIN

Has a pink patch around its eyes.

6. LITTLE SPOTTED KIWI

Its nostrils are at the tip of the beak, giving it an excellent sense of smell.

7. ROCKHOPPER PENGUIN

Hops from rock to rock to reach the tops of cliffs.

8. YELLOW-EYED PENGUIN

Does not burrow but nests in forests.

FLIGHTLESS BIRDS have, over millions of years, found they no longer need to take to the sky. Some use their wings as flippers to propel them through water.

Key

1. SOUTHERN CASSOWARY ....

The southern cassowary uses its gray casque (growth on its head) to push through dense rainforest vegetation. Its head and neck are blue, its wattles red, and its body is black.

2. FAIRY PENGUIN ....

Found along the coasts of New Zealand and southern Australia, fairy penguins are the smallest penguin species. They nest in an underground burrow. Their backs and heads are blue-gray, and their feet, pink.

3. EMU ....

The emu's grayish-brown plumage resembles coarse hair and hides tiny wings, which they flap when running. It is believed this stabilizes the bird. They eat seeds, berries, and insects.

4. EMPEROR PENGUIN ....

Black and yellow emperors are the only penguins that breed during winter. Males keep a single egg warm by covering it with a furry flap of skin and huddling together, enduring temperatures as low as minus 80° F.

5. JACKASS PENGUIN ....

Jackass penguins inhabit rocky ground on the southernmost coasts of South Africa and nearby islands. They have a pink patch around their eyes, black backs and wings, and a white underside.

6. LITTLE SPOTTED KIWI ....

Kiwis have their nostrils located at the tip of the beak, giving them an excellent sense of smell as they search for earthworms and insects at night. They have irregular bands of brown feathers and a cream beak.

7. ROCKHOPPER PENGUIN ....

The rockhopper penguin is named for its ability to jump from rock to rock to reach the tops of cliffs, where it nests close to other seabirds. Their distinctive crests are black and yellow, and their feet are pink.

8. YELLOW-EYED PENGUIN ....

Classed as the rarest of penguins, the yellow-eyed penguin does not use a burrow but retreats into nearby forests to nest. This makes both adults and young vulnerable to predators. Their beaks are reddish-purple.

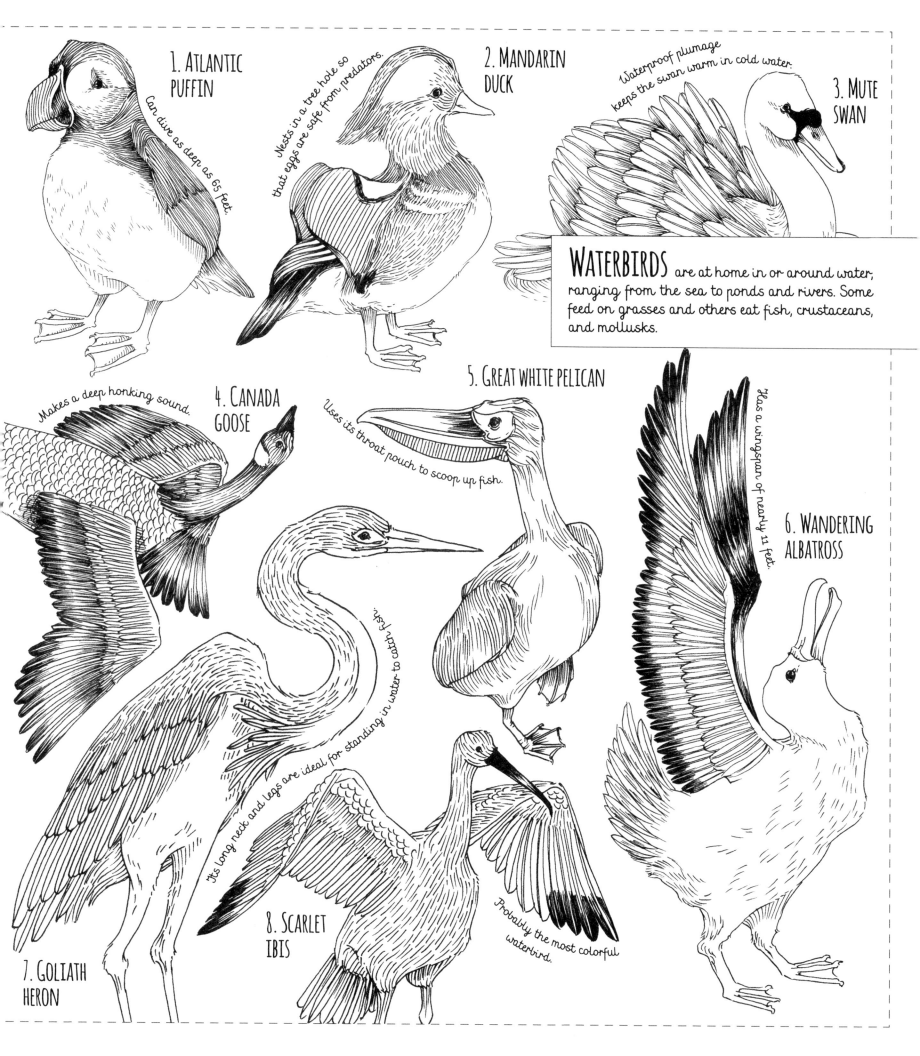

1. ATLANTIC PUFFIN

Can dive as deep as 65 feet.

2. MANDARIN DUCK

Nests in a tree hole so that eggs are safe from predators.

3. MUTE SWAN

Waterproof plumage keeps the swan warm in cold water.

WATERBIRDS are at home in or around water, ranging from the sea to ponds and rivers. Some feed on grasses and others eat fish, crustaceans, and mollusks.

4. CANADA GOOSE

Makes a deep honking sound.

5. GREAT WHITE PELICAN

Uses its throat pouch to scoop up fish.

6. WANDERING ALBATROSS

Has a wingspan of nearly 11 feet.

7. GOLIATH HERON

Its long neck and legs are ideal for standing in water to catch fish.

8. SCARLET IBIS

Probably the most colorful waterbird.

KEY

1. ATLANTIC PUFFIN ....

Part of the Atlantic puffin's red, yellow, and blue beak is shed in winter, and grows back during the breeding season. It speeds through water, diving as deep as 65 feet. Its wings and back are black, and the body is white.

2. MANDARIN DUCK ....

The Mandarin duck is unusual in that it nests in tree holes so that eggs are safe from predators. Its ducklings leap from the nest hole to the water or ground below. It has green sides and orange wings.

3. MUTE SWAN ....

Despite its name ("mute" means "silent"), mute swans make several calls, including a snake-like hiss when threatened. Waterproof white plumage keeps them warm in cold water. Their beaks are orange.

4. CANADA GOOSE ....

Canada geese make deep honking sounds. Some migrate, flying distances of almost a thousand miles, but some stay in one area throughout the year. Their heads and necks are black, and their bodies are brown.

5. GREAT WHITE PELICAN ....

The great white pelican is one of the heaviest flying waterbirds. It uses its throat pouch to scoop up fish and store regurgitated food for its chicks to feed on. As its name suggests, it is white, but it has pink legs.

6. WANDERING ALBATROSS ....

Long, narrow wings spanning nearly 11 feet enable the wandering albatross to use strong winds and fly effortlessly for long distances. It is white with black mottled wings and pink feet.

7. GOLIATH HERON ....

The Goliath heron's short tail, long chestnut neck, and long legs are ideal for standing in water for extended periods waiting for fish, which it stabs with its dagger-shaped beak. Its back and wings are gray.

8. SCARLET IBIS ....

Probably the most colorful waterbird, the scarlet ibis lives in tropical river mouths and mudflats, nesting in mangrove trees. It uses its highly sensitive black beak to feel for food in muddy waters.

1. BATELEUR EAGLE

The name "bateleur" is French for "acrobat."

Watches for other species to spot food before descending.

3. HARPY EAGLE

Can pluck monkeys and sloths from trees.

2. KING VULTURE

So sensitive to sound it can hear a mouse moving through the grass.

5. SPECTACLED OWL

Hunts roosting birds and small mammals at night.

BIRDS OF PREY are mainly solitary hunters, with large eyes; strong, hooked beaks, and sharp talons for grasping the unfortunate creatures that they feed on.

4. BARN OWL

Also known as the fishing eagle.

Its legs and toes are feathered to protect it from snow and ice.

A fast runner; hunts prey on the ground.

6. BALD EAGLE

8. SNOWY OWL

7. SECRETARY BIRD

KEY

1. BATELEUR EAGLE

The name "bateleur" is French for "acrobat." This red and black eagle produces flight displays of rolling and rocking from side to side. Sometimes, it will halt with its wings wide open, while still in mid-air.

2. KING VULTURE

The king vulture watches for other species to spot carrion (dead animals) before descending and using its sharp talons and a strong beak to tear flesh apart. It has a white chest and black back and wings.

3. HARPY EAGLE

One of the largest and most powerful species, the harpy eagle plucks monkeys and sloths from trees in the early morning before the mammals wake up. It has a gray head, black back and wings, and yellow feet.

4. BARN OWL

Barn owls are so sensitive to sound they are able to hear a mouse moving through the grass. Like other species of owl, they fly silently, mostly at night. Their faces and chests are white and their wings tawny.

5. SPECTACLED OWL

Orange eyes surrounded by dark feathers with white markings above and below, create the effect of spectacles (eye glasses). At night, it flies from tree to tree, hunting roosting birds and small mammals.

6. BALD EAGLE

The bald eagle is also known as the fishing eagle. Its feet are featherless so that they don't become waterlogged and heavy when snatching prey from the water's surface. Its head and neck are white and its beak yellow.

7. SECRETARY BIRD

A fast runner, the secretary bird is an unusual bird of prey—it hunts snakes, small rodents, and insects on the ground. It has orange cheeks, a pale gray chest, dark gray back and wings, and a black head crest.

8. SNOWY OWL

Snowy owls become whiter as they age. Their legs and toes are heavily feathered to protect them from snow and ice. Hunting at dawn and dusk, these owls feed on small rodents, fish, frogs, and crabs.

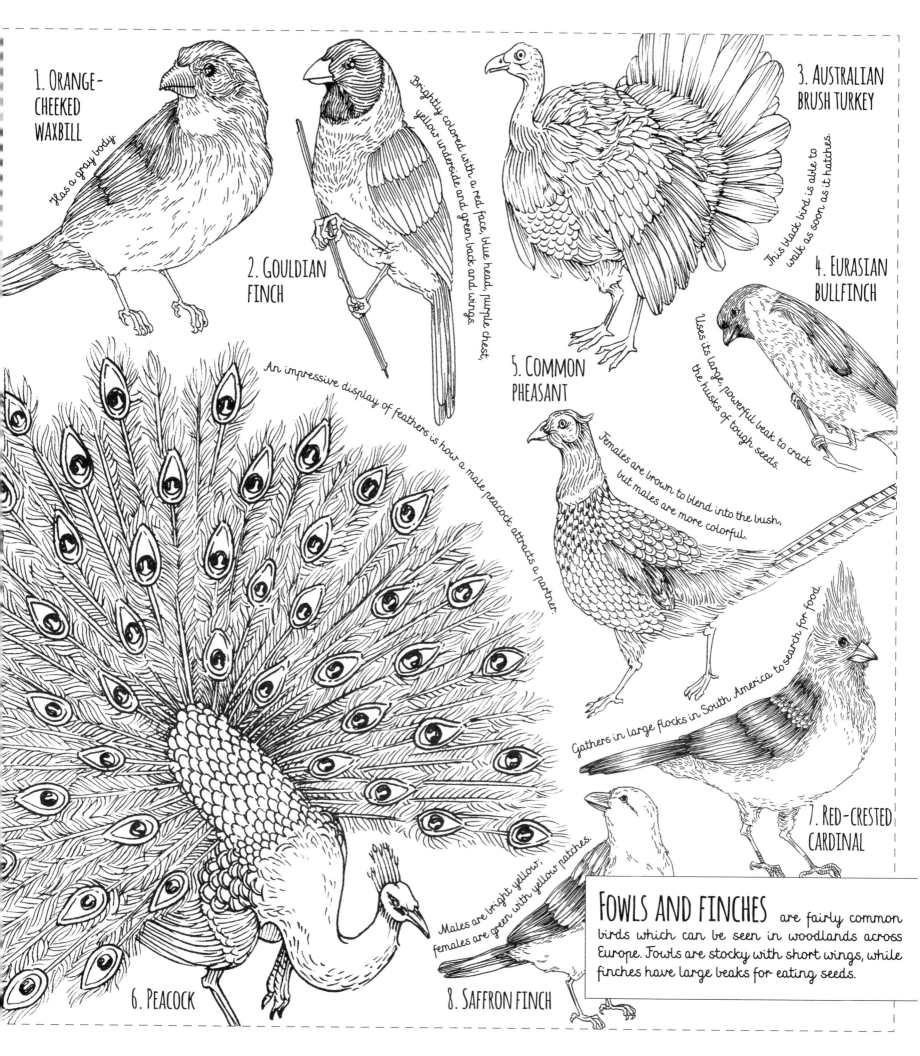

1. ORANGE-CHEEKED WAXBILL

Has a gray body.

2. GOULDIAN FINCH

Brightly colored with a red face, blue head, purple chest, yellow underside and green back and wings.

3. AUSTRALIAN BRUSH TURKEY

This black bird is able to walk as soon as it hatches.

4. EURASIAN BULLFINCH

Uses its large, powerful beak to crack the husks of tough seeds.

5. COMMON PHEASANT

Females are brown to blend into the bush, but males are more colorful.

An impressive display of feathers is how a male peacock attracts a partner.

Gathers in large flocks in South America to search for food.

7. RED-CRESTED CARDINAL

6. PEACOCK

Males are bright yellow; females are green with yellow patches.

8. SAFFRON FINCH

FOWLS AND FINCHES are fairly common birds which can be seen in woodlands across Europe. Fowls are stocky with short wings, while finches have large beaks for eating seeds.

KEY

1. ORANGE-CHEEKED WAXBILL ....

This bird gets its name from the orange patches on its cheeks. It has brown wings, a gray body, and a red beak. Orange-cheeked waxbills pair for life. A male courts a female by hopping up and down in front of her.

2. GOULDIAN FINCH ....

The gaudy-colored gouldian finch feeds on grass seeds all year. During dry spells, it supplements this diet with small insects. It is endangered because much of its habitat has been turned into fields for cattle.

3. AUSTRALIAN BRUSH TURKEY ....

Male brush turkeys use their large feet to scrape together a mound of leaves and other vegetation, which they use to keep the females' eggs warm. They have black bodies, red heads, and yellow wattles.

4. EURASIAN BULLFINCH ....

The Eurasian bullfinch has bright red cheeks, a gray body, and a large, powerful beak that it uses for cracking the husks of tough seeds. It is a shy bird, living in pairs in woodland, but you might sometimes see it in gardens.

5. COMMON PHEASANT ....

At night, pheasants roost in bushes to keep safe. The plumage of male pheasants is bright purple and brown, with a white ring around their necks, but females are brown to blend in with their surroundings.

6. PEACOCK ....

The male peacock, also called peafowl, has a long train of green feathers with blue, green, and copper eyespots. He will open this into a fan to attract a mate. Powerful feet are used to scratch for insects and seeds.

7. RED-CRESTED CARDINAL ....

Red-crested cardinals are named for their bright red heads, crests, and throats. They have white fronts, and gray wings and backs. Young cardinals that have left the nest continue to be cared for by the males.

8. SAFFRON FINCH ....

Male saffron finches are bright yellow, but females are greener, with yellow patches. A sociable bird, the saffron finch will gather in large numbers in open, shrubby areas to hunt for seeds.

Has sky-blue wings and a pale blue underside.

1. MOUNTAIN BLUEBIRD

Is heard rather than seen.

2. ICTERINE WARBLER

Has a habit of holding its tail in an upright position.

3. SPLENDID FAIRY WREN

Males mark their territory with loud, musical songs.

4. ROSE-BREASTED GROSBEAK

Delivers a thin, high-pitched song.

5. BLACKBURNIAN WARBLER

SONGBIRDS have the instinct to sing from the moment they hatch. They communicate in many musical ways, from simple calls or squawks to a complex series of notes.

Likes to eat snails by smashing them against a rock to break the shell.

6. SONG THRUSH

Was once kept as a cage bird because of the musical notes it produces.

7. COMMON LINNET

Searches for food in moss and in the water.

8. GRAY WAGTAIL

Key

1. MOUNTAIN BLUEBIRD ....

The brilliantly colored male mountain bluebird—which has sky-blue wings and pale blue underparts—chooses a high-up spot in its forest habitat from which to sing a rich, warbling song.

2. ICTERINE WARBLER ....

The icterine warbler is heard rather than seen. Its dark brown-green wings and head conceal it among bushes and trees while it sends out a melodious and long-lasting song.

3. SPLENDID FAIRY WREN ....

The splendid fairy wren has a habit of holding its tail in an upright position. Its plumage, attractive to females in breeding season, is cobalt blue with paler blue cheek patches and a black band across its chest and face.

4. ROSE-BREASTED GROSBEAK ....

Male rose-breasted grosbeaks are very territorial. They announce their presence with loud, musical songs. They have black heads and backs, and get their name from their rose-pink chests.

5. BLACKBURNIAN WARBLER ....

From the tops of trees, the male blackburnian warbler delivers a thin, high-pitched song. It has a black face mask with a yellow band, a vivid orange throat, a yellow belly, and white and black panels on its wings.

6. SONG THRUSH ....

This brown and cream bird announces its presence with a series of loud, clear, ringing tones. It will pick up a snail with its beak and smash it against a stone to break the shell and get the soft mollusk inside.

7. COMMON LINNET ....

During the breeding season, the pale red forehead and pink chest of the male linnet become more intensely colored. This bird was once kept as a cage bird because of the musical notes it produces.

8. GRAY WAGTAIL ....

The gray wagtail spends much of its time close to water. It searches for food in mosses and in the water, scouring for insects and their larvae. It has slate-gray upperparts, while its underside is bright yellow.

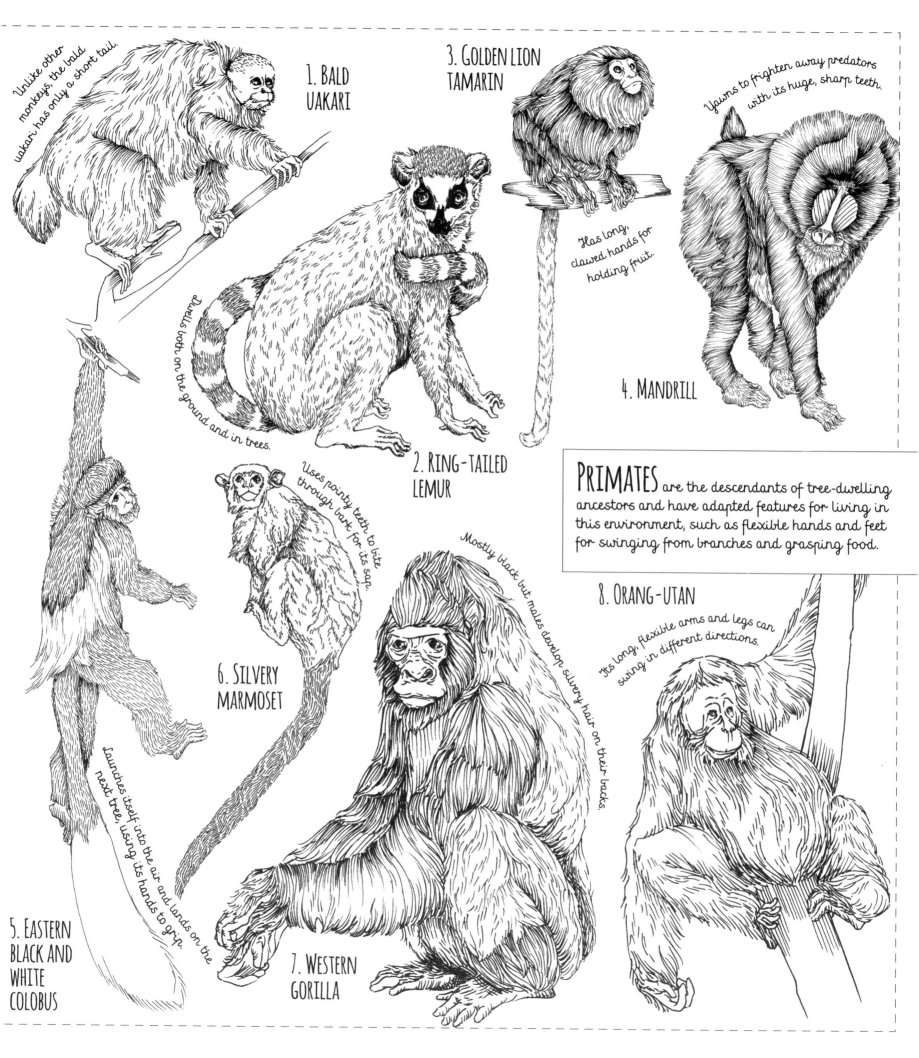

Unlike other monkeys, the bald uakari has only a short tail.

1. BALD UAKARI

3. GOLDEN LION TAMARIN

Yawns to frighten away predators with its huge, sharp teeth.

Has long, clawed hands for holding fruit.

4. MANDRILL

Dwells both on the ground and in trees.

2. RING-TAILED LEMUR

Uses pointy teeth to bite through bark for its sap.

PRIMATES are the descendants of tree-dwelling ancestors and have adapted features for living in this environment, such as flexible hands and feet for swinging from branches and grasping food.

8. ORANG-UTAN

Its long, flexible arms and legs can swing in different directions.

6. SILVERY MARMOSET

Mostly black but males develop silvery hair on their backs.

Launches itself into the air and lands on the next tree, using its hands to grip.

5. EASTERN BLACK AND WHITE COLOBUS

7. WESTERN GORILLA

Key

1. **Bald uakari** ....

This monkey has reddish-brown fur with a bright red, hairless face. Despite having only a short tail, the bald uakari is very agile in its treetop home, unlike other monkeys. When excited, it wags its stumpy tail.

2. **Ring-tailed lemur** ....

Black and white ring-tailed lemurs dwell both on the ground and in trees. A group of about twenty hunt during the day using their hands to gather fruit, nuts, and leaves. Their upper bodies are brownish-gray.

3. **Golden lion tamarin** ....

Long, clawed hands are used by the golden lion tamarin for holding fruit and poking into tree bark to find grub. It has a dark gray face; golden-orange head and body, and brown feet.

4. **Mandrill** ....

Mandrills live on the forest floor in troops of about 250, searching for fruits, seeds, eggs, and insects. They have bright red noses and blue cheeks, and yawn to display huge, sharp teeth, frightening away predators.

5. **Eastern black and white colobus** ....

Galloping along branches, these monkeys launch themselves into the air to land on the next tree, using hook-like hands to grip. They are black with white borders on their faces and white veils on their bodies.

6. **Silvery marmoset** ....

Marmosets feed on fruit, leaves, and insects, and have pointed bottom teeth that they use to pierce tree bark and lick out the sap. They have pale silvery fur on their backs, black tails, and cream bodies.

7. **Western gorilla** ....

Gorillas are mostly black but males develop silvery white hair on their backs. If threatened, a male hoots loudly, beats his chest, and throws vegetation before knocking down the enemy with a hand swipe.

8. **Orang-utan** ....

Long, flexible arms, and legs that can swing in different directions, enable orang-utans to spend most of their lives in the forest canopy, swinging from tree to tree. Their coats are burgundy and their faces orange.

1. AFRICAN ELEPHANT

Its humps store fat to be used by the body when food is scarce.

3. GEMSBOK

2. BACTRIAN CAMEL

Doesn't sweat or pant until the temperature reaches 113°F.

The largest land mammal in the world.

Can't see well, but has good hearing and sense of smell.

LARGE HERBIVORES live in grasslands and bordering forests, where they graze on grasses, shrubs, and trees. Food and water can be scarce, so these animals have cleverly adapted to survive.

4. OKAPI

7. GIRAFFE

5. HIPPOPOTAMUS

Able to float by filling its lungs with air.

Capable of bursts of speed when threatened.

A long neck helps it find foods out of the reach of other creatures.

Its horns can grow to 5 feet.

6. WHITE RHINOCEROS

8. GREATER KUDU

KEY

1. AFRICAN ELEPHANT
The huge, light gray body of the African elephant—the largest land animal—is supported by pillar-like legs. The trunk is adaptable, able to pick up a nut with the lips or lift a heavy log with the whole trunk.

2. BACTRIAN CAMEL
The Bactrian camel is found in only a few areas in the wild. Fat is stored in the humps and used by the body when food is scarce. They are pale-beige in color with dark brown beards and tufts on their heads.

3. GEMSBOK
To go for several days without water in hot areas of the savanna, the gemsbok doesn't sweat or pant until the temperature is 113°F. It has a gray body with black and white markings.

4. OKAPI
Although unable to see well, the okapi has acute hearing and sense of smell, which it needs to survive its solitary life in the forest. Its coat is a dark reddish-brown, but it has white stripes on its legs and rump, like a zebra.

5. HIPPOPOTAMUS
Hippopotamuses live in herds of about 40, spending the day in water to stay cool. By filling their lungs with air their dark gray bodies are able to float. Their undersides are pink, as is the skin around their eyes.

6. WHITE RHINOCEROS
White rhinos are actually slate-gray to yellowish-brown in color. They are the third heaviest mammals but are capable of bursts of speed when threatened. The wide mouth is ideal for cropping grass.

7. GIRAFFE
The tan-colored giraffe's long neck, marked distinctively with brown patches, enables it to retrieve foods out of the reach of other creatures. It grasps leaves off the acacia tree with its 17-inch tongue.

8. GREATER KUDU
One of the largest antelopes, with horns that grow to over five feet, is the grayish-red greater kudu. The spiral shape of its horns allows it to lock horns with other males during fighting contests.

A tawny coat provides camouflage when hiding in long, dry grasses.

Can run at 60 miles per hour for up to a minute when chasing prey.

2. Cheetah

1. Lion

Cats have muscular bodies; strong, sharp teeth and claws; and an excellent sense of smell, sight (including night vision), and hearing. They are formidable, carnivorous hunters.

Hunts at night for small mammals and reptiles.

3. Sand cat

4. Margay

Can rotate its feet 180 degrees to hang upside down.

5. Snow leopard

6. Andean cat

Large, furry paws help it to walk on snow and ice.

Long, thick fur provides insulation for cold nights in the mountains.

Every tiger has a different striped pattern.

Olive-gray coat helps to camouflage it in water.

7. Tiger

8. Fishing cat

KEY

1. LION

Lions are the only cats to live in groups known as prides, working together to kill prey much larger than themselves. Their tawny coats provide excellent camouflage for hiding in long, dry grasses.

2. CHEETAH

Cheetahs can run at 60 miles an hour for up to a minute while attempting to catch gazelles and grazing cattle. Their distinctive coats are yellowish-brown with small black spots.

3. SAND CAT

The sand cat is a pale grayish-brown with yellow eyes. It manages to live in very dry areas, drinking hardly any water, getting moisture from its food. It hunts at night for small mammals and reptiles.

4. MARGAY

The margay spends its time in trees, where its cream, dark-brown-spotted coat matches the dappled light. It is the only cat that can rotate its hind feet 180 degrees so it can hang upside-down and descend tree trunks easily.

5. SNOW LEOPARD

The snow leopard lives in rocky, often snow-covered mountains. Its cream-colored, dense fur coat (with distinctive black rosettes) keeps it warm, while large, furry paws help it to walk on snow and ice.

6. ANDEAN CAT

Living in the mountains, the long, thick, gray-brown fur of the Andean cat provides insulation for cold nights in the winter. The solitary animal hunts for small rodents such as chinchillas and viscachas.

7. TIGER

The largest of the cat family, the striped pattern on the tiger's bright orange coat allows it to blend into dense, shaded vegetation so it can creep up on prey undetected. Every tiger has a different pattern.

8. FISHING CAT

With slightly webbed toes, the fishing cat is a semi-aquatic hunter. Tapping the water's surface to attract fish, it uses a paw to scoop them out. Its olive-gray coat —with black spots—helps it blend in with the water.

1. WILD ASS

Has been used to carry heavy loads for 6,000 years.

2. PRZEWALSKI'S HORSE

Its reddish-brown coat becomes paler in winter to help it blend in with the snowy background.

4. ARABIAN HORSE

Lives in Asian deserts where food can be scarce, so occasionally forages for locusts.

3. TARPAN

Became extinct in the late 1800s.

HORSES are herding creatures, famous for their size, speed, and agility. Erect ears and eyes at the sides of the head provide an acute sense of hearing and sight, to detect danger.

Lives in herds of about 400.

Can reach speeds of 43 miles per hour.

5. KIANG

7. MONGOLIAN WILD ASS

Has a larger head than other asses.

Each zebra has its own distinctive pattern.

6. GREVY'S ZEBRA

8. ONAGER

Key

1. Wild ass .... Wild asses are strong and sure-footed and have been used to carry heavy loads over rough ground for over 6,000 years. Their coats are gray with white underparts and black bands on their lower legs.

2. Przewalski's horse .... In winter, the reddish-brown coat of the Przewalski's horse becomes thicker, paler and longer to help the horse keep warm and blend into the snowy background. It lives in herds, wandering across areas of grassland.

3. Tarpan .... The light gray tarpan—which became extinct in the late 1800s—has the same scientific name as "wild horse." All light-colored horses have descended from the tarpan. Its mane and legs are black.

4. Arabian horse .... For 4,500 years, the Arabian horse has been valued for its speed and stamina. It lives in Asian deserts where grass can be scarce, so occasionally it forages for locusts and dates. It is light gray with a black mane.

5. Kiang .... The kiang is a type of ass from Tibet that lives in herds of about 400. During the breeding season, the stallions fight each other to gain control over the herd. Their coats are white with a red head, back, and rump.

6. Grevy's zebra .... The Grevy's zebra has a black and white pattern that dazzles predators when it's running away. Each zebra has distinctive markings, which helps different members of the group recognize each other.

7. Mongolian wild ass .... The Mongolian wild ass has a larger head than other asses and a sandy yellow coat with a black tail, dark gray mane, and black stripe along its spine. It moves about in herds, searching for vegetation.

8. Onager .... Living in areas of Iran where water is scarce, herds of onager need to move around the inhospitable terrain quickly and can reach speeds of 43 miles per hour over short distances. Their coats are pale yellow.

1. AXIS DEER

Dashes for cover when predators are detected.

2. ALPINE IBEX

lives in the mountains of the European Alps.

3. MARKHOR

Its horns are prized by hunters, meaning this creature is now scarce.

4. WARTHOG

Has padded wrists to protect its forelegs.

SMALL HERBIVORES feed on grasses and plants. They are often preyed upon by larger, carnivorous animals; as a result, they have developed a keen sense for detecting danger.

5. BUSH PIG

Has a dark brown coat with white hair on its cheeks.

6. THOMSON'S GAZELLE

Often preyed upon by large cats.

7. BARBARY SHEEP

Avoids feeding at midday when temperatures are high.

8. MALAYAN TAPIR

Uses its trunk as a snorkel when submerged in water.

KEY

1. AXIS DEER ·······················

Axis deer live in herds of about a hundred. They will dash for cover when predators are detected, reaching speeds of forty miles per hour. Their coats are reddish-brown with lines of white spots.

2. ALPINE IBEX ·······················

The brown Alpine ibex lives in the mountains of the European Alps. Food is scarce, so it will climb steep cliffs in search of plants to eat. The female (pictured here) has horns that are smaller and less curved than the male's.

3. MARKHOR ·······················

The spiraling gray horns of the markhor can be five feet long in males. Markhors are prized by hunters, which is why this majestic creature is now endangered. Their coats are reddish-gray and the lower legs are white.

4. WARTHOG ·······················

Feeding mainly on grasses, the warthog has padded wrists to protect its forelegs when it kneels to graze. The warts that cover its head are actually protective bumps. It has a brown body and yellow tusks.

5. BUSH PIG ·······················

Resting during the day in its underground burrow, the bush pig emerges at night to feed on grasses, leaves, eggs, birds, and small lizards. It has a dark brown coat with a black snout and white hair on its cheeks.

6. THOMSON'S GAZELLE ·······················

The small Thomson's gazelle has a sandy-colored coat with a dark stripe on its side, a black tail, and white underparts. It gathers in large herds to graze on grass and is often preyed upon by large cats.

7. BARBARY SHEEP ·······················

Barbary sheep live in semi-desert areas where they forage for plants, avoiding feeding at midday when temperatures are high. Their coats are yellow with a red tinge and their curved horns are reddish-gray.

8. MALAYAN TAPIR ·······················

The Malayan tapir is black with a large white patch. This breaks up its outline in shady forests, helping it to stay hidden. It is often submerged in water, using its short trunk as a snorkel.

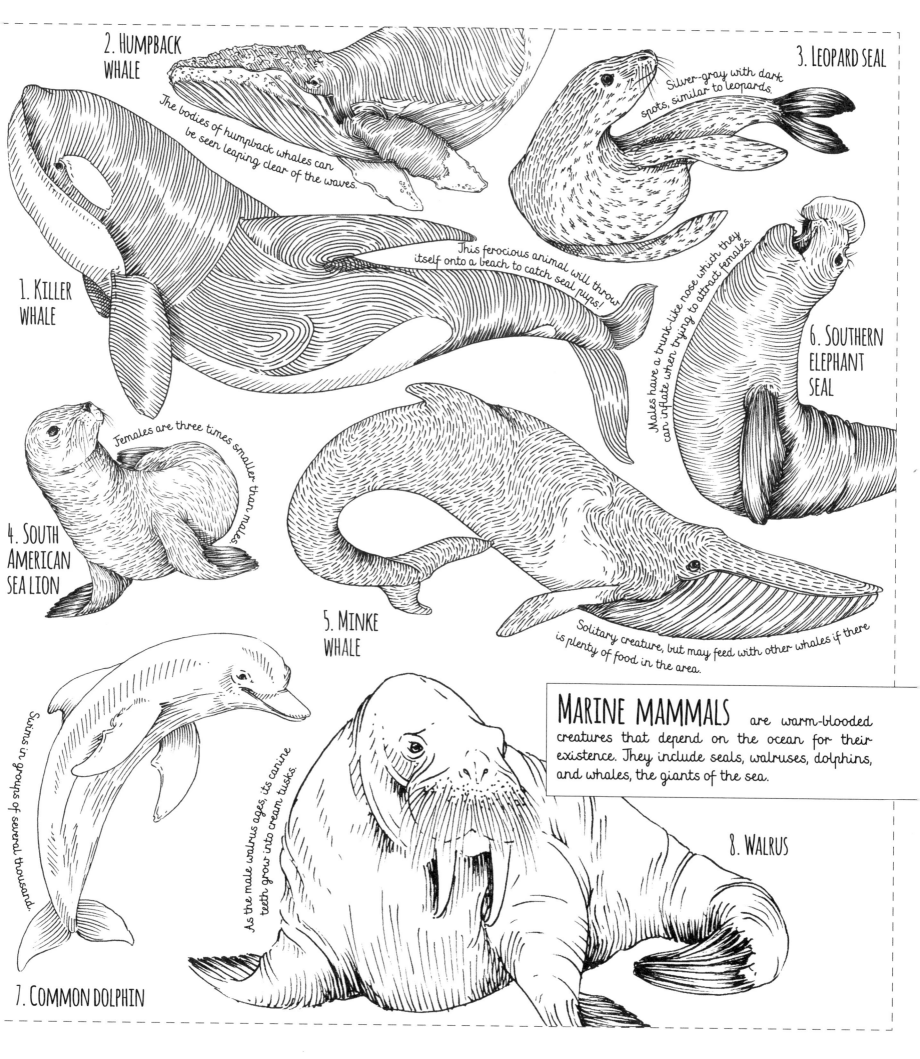

2. HUMPBACK WHALE

The bodies of humpback whales can be seen leaping clear of the waves.

3. LEOPARD SEAL

Silver-gray with dark spots, similar to leopards.

This ferocious animal will throw itself onto a beach to catch seal pups!

Males have a trunk-like nose which they can inflate when trying to attract females.

1. KILLER WHALE

6. SOUTHERN ELEPHANT SEAL

4. SOUTH AMERICAN SEA LION

Females are three times smaller than males.

5. MINKE WHALE

Solitary creature, but may feed with other whales if there is plenty of food in the area.

Swims in groups of several thousand.

As the male walrus ages, its canine teeth grow into cream tusks.

MARINE MAMMALS are warm-blooded creatures that depend on the ocean for their existence. They include seals, walruses, dolphins, and whales, the giants of the sea.

8. WALRUS

7. COMMON DOLPHIN

Key

1. Killer whale ....

Herding fish, tipping over ice floes to knock seals and penguins into the water, and even throwing themselves onto a beach to catch seal pups are all hunting methods used by the ferocious black and white killer whale.

2. Humpback whale ....

The blueish-black bodies of humpback whales can be seen breaching—leaping clear of the waves. They communicate by tail-and-flipper slapping, rolling, and spy-hopping (holding their heads briefly above water).

3. Leopard seal ....

With similar markings to land leopards, these seals are silvery-gray with darker spots. They feed on other seals and penguins, holding them with the claws on their flippers and biting to kill with their large, sharp teeth.

4. South American sea lion ....

South American sea lions have brown fur with light brown to yellow underbellies. A male South American sea lion is about three times larger than a female (pictured here) and has a thick shoulder and chest mane.

5. Minke whale ....

Usually solitary, the minke whale may occasionally feed with other whales if there is plenty of food in the area. They have a black head, back, and tail, with grayish sides and white undersides.

6. Southern elephant seal ....

The silvery-gray male southern elephant seals have a trunk-like nose which can be inflated when trying to attract a group of females. They dive continuously, staying underwater for about 20 minutes per dive.

7. Common dolphin ....

Common dolphins are often found in groups of several thousand. As the gray dolphins swim, they communicate by clicking, squeaking, and croaking. Unlike whales, dolphins only have one blowhole.

8. Walrus ....

As they age, the canine teeth of the male walrus grow to become cream tusks. The sensitive whiskers around their snouts help them find mussels and clams in rocky sediment. Their bodies are brown with a pink tinge.

1. GREEN SEA TURTLE

Has powerful flippers for swimming.

2. GALÁPAGOS TORTOISE

The largest living tortoise, growing to four feet.

Eats dead animals, crunching bones to get calcium.

4. SIDE-NECKED TURTLE

Its long neck helps the turtle grab at prey.

5. INDIAN STARRED TORTOISE

3. RED-FOOTED TORTOISE

TURTLES AND TORTOISES are the oldest living reptiles. They are easily recognized by their shells, which protect their soft body parts. These shells come in many patterns and shapes.

Prefers the humid monsoon season.

Breathes through its snout when swimming.

7. ALLIGATOR SNAPPING TURTLE

6. SPINY SOFT-SHELLED TURTLE

Its flexible shell helps the tortoise clamber over rocks.

Its brown color and algae on its shell make it look like a log.

8. PANCAKE TORTOISE

KEY

1. GREEN SEA TURTLE ....

A streamlined shell and powerful flippers help the green sea turtle migrate over 600 miles, from feeding grounds to breeding beaches. The carapace (shell) is green with a brownish tinge.

2. GALÁPAGOS TORTOISE ....

The largest living tortoise—growing to 550 pounds—the Galápagos tortoise has a huge shell, long neck, and massive limbs to bear its weight. Its shell is yellowish-brown and it has brown scales on its body.

3. RED-FOOTED TORTOISE ....

As well as feeding on plants and fruit, the red-footed tortoise will eat carrion (dead animals), crunching bones to get extra calcium, which helps its shell grow. It is brown with red scales on its legs and feet.

4. SIDE-NECKED TURTLE ....

The side-necked turtle lives in or near water. Its long neck helps it grab at passing prey and can become a snorkel, breathing air when the creature is resting in shallow water. Its shell is dark brown or black.

5. INDIAN STARRED TORTOISE ....

Unlike many other species, the Indian starred tortoise likes to drink, and prefers the humid monsoon season to the dry season, where it is less active. The distinctive knobbly shell is black with yellow lines.

6. SPINY SOFT-SHELLED TURTLE ....

The spiny, soft-shelled turtle is a strong swimmer, often cruising underwater and breathing through its snorkel-like snout. It is tan in color, with a yellow line on each side of its head and a yellow edge to its shell.

7. ALLIGATOR SNAPPING TURTLE ....

Sitting on the bottom of a pond, the alligator snapping turtle's brown shell resembles a log. It opens its mouth to reveal a pink worm-like piece of flesh. This acts as a lure, attracting fish, which are snapped up by powerful jaws.

8. PANCAKE TORTOISE ....

The pale brown carapace of the pancake tortoise is flat and flexible, allowing the reptile to clamber over rocks and wedge itself into narrow crevices to escape attackers. Its head and feet are yellow.

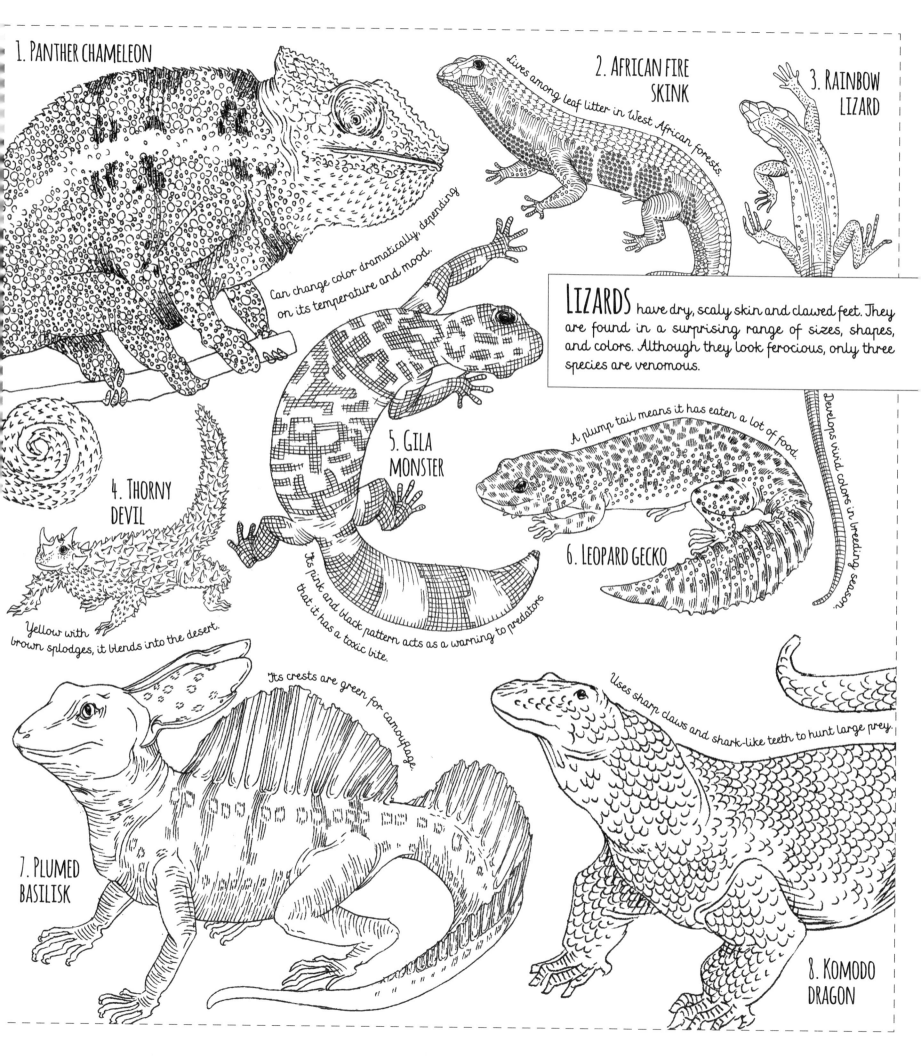

1. PANTHER CHAMELEON

2. AFRICAN FIRE SKINK

Lives among leaf litter in West African forests.

3. RAINBOW LIZARD

Can change color dramatically, depending on its temperature and mood.

LIZARDS have dry, scaly skin and clawed feet. They are found in a surprising range of sizes, shapes, and colors. Although they look ferocious, only three species are venomous.

5. GILA MONSTER

A plump tail means it has eaten a lot of food.

Develops vivid colors in breeding season.

4. THORNY DEVIL

6. LEOPARD GECKO

Yellow with brown splodges, it blends into the desert.

Its pink and black pattern acts as a warning to predators that it has a toxic bite.

Its crests are green for camouflage.

Uses sharp claws and shark-like teeth to hunt large prey.

7. PLUMED BASILISK

8. KOMODO DRAGON

KEY

1. PANTHER CHAMELEON
....

Chameleons can change color dramatically depending on their temperature and mood. This is how they communicate with each other. All panther chameleons have a long tongue for catching prey.

2. AFRICAN FIRE SKINK
....

The African fire skink has a red face and chest and a brown body with black and red bands. It lives among leaf litter in West African forests. If attacked, it can shed its tail to distract the predator and get away.

3. RAINBOW LIZARD
....

In breeding season, the male rainbow lizard develops an orange head, blue body and tail, and red front legs. It finds a raised spot and makes a head-bobbing display to attract a female mate.

4. THORNY DEVIL
....

The thorny devil is yellow with brown splotches. It moves slowly through the desert, blending into the background. If any predators spot it and attack, the spines on its back provide good protection.

5. GILA MONSTER
....

A pink-and-black pattern acts as a warning sign to predators that the Gila monster has a toxic bite. It also provides camouflage when the lizard is resting in the dappled shadows of desert scrub.

6. LEOPARD GECKO
....

This lizard gets its name from its yellow-and-black coloring, which is similar to that of a leopard. Its back and tail are covered in tiny warts. If the leopard gecko has eaten lots of food, its tail will be really plump.

7. PLUMED BASILISK
....

Only male plumed basilisks have crests on their heads, bodies and tails, which are colored green for camouflage. When threatened, the basilisks can drop into water and run across the surface on their hind legs.

8. KOMODO DRAGON
....

The heaviest lizard, the Komodo dragon uses its sharp claws and shark-like teeth to hunt large prey, such as deer and water buffalo. It is grayish-brown with a red or yellow tinge to its scales.

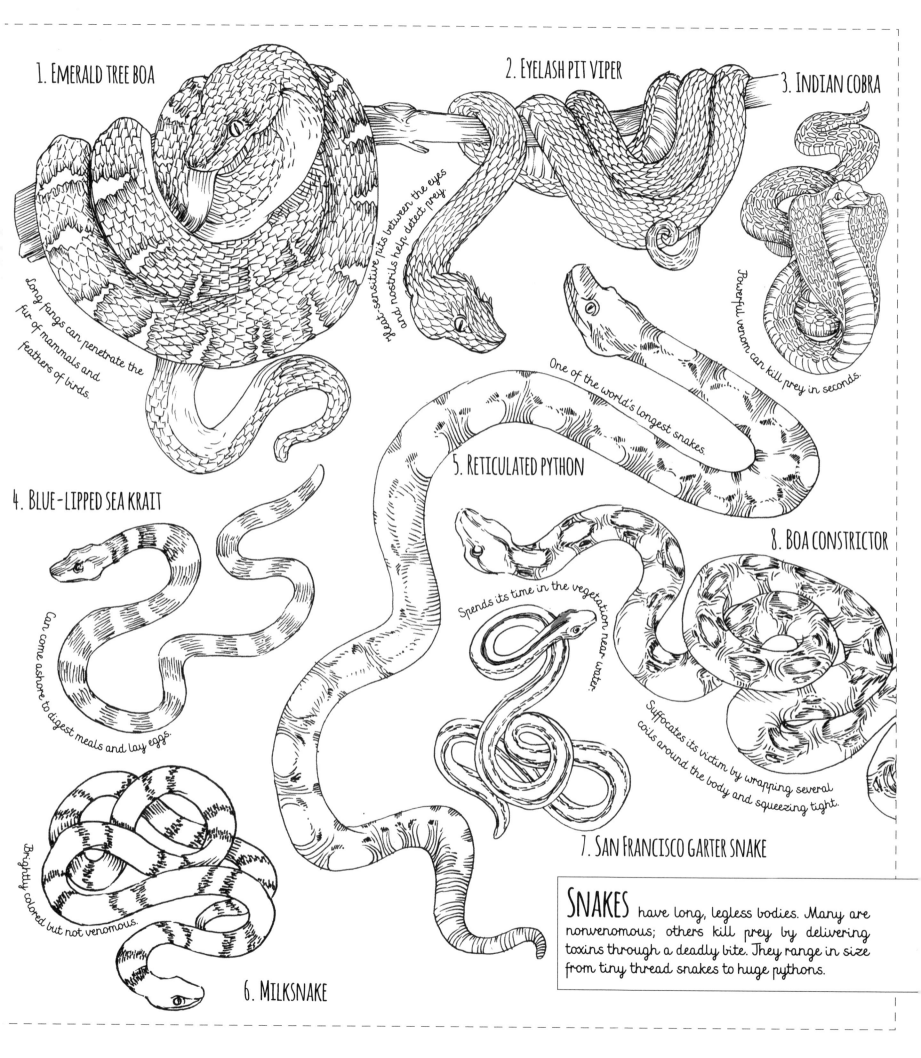

1. EMERALD TREE BOA

2. EYELASH PIT VIPER

3. INDIAN COBRA

Long fangs can penetrate the fur of mammals and feathers of birds.

Heat-sensitive pits between the eyes and nostrils help detect prey.

Powerful venom can kill prey in seconds.

One of the world's longest snakes.

5. RETICULATED PYTHON

4. BLUE-LIPPED SEA KRAIT

8. BOA CONSTRICTOR

Can come ashore to digest meals and lay eggs.

Spends its time in the vegetation near water.

Suffocates its victim by wrapping several coils around the body and squeezing tight.

7. SAN FRANCISCO GARTER SNAKE

Brightly colored but not venomous.

6. MILKSNAKE

SNAKES have long, legless bodies. Many are nonvenomous; others kill prey by delivering toxins through a deadly bite. They range in size from tiny thread snakes to huge pythons.

KEY

1. EMERALD TREE BOA ....

Emerald tree boas are arboreal (tree-dwelling); they drape their coils around branches. They have long fangs for penetrating the fur of mammals and the feathers of birds. Their name comes from their vibrant green color.

2. EYELASH PIT VIPER ....

The golden-yellow eyelash pit viper has long, hinged fangs and a pair of heat-sensitive pits between its nostrils and eyes. These detect prey; sensing the location, as well as the distance, of a potential meal.

3. INDIAN COBRA ....

When the Indian cobra is threatened and expands its "hood" in defense, the attacker sees the intimidating black band across the snake's neck. A powerful bite can kill a lizard, a bird, even a small mammal—in seconds.

4. BLUE-LIPPED SEA KRAIT ....

Its well-developed muscles allow the blue-lipped sea krait to come ashore—unlike other sea snakes—to regurgitate its meals and lay its eggs. It is striped blue-and-black and has a black head with a white nose.

5. RETICULATED PYTHON ....

Regarded as one of the world's longest snakes, the reticulated python feeds on large mammals and birds, killing them by constriction. It is olive-green with black and yellow markings.

6. MILKSNAKE ....

Although milk snakes are brightly colored—with red, black, and white/yellow bands—they are not venomous. Secretive and nocturnal, they feed on lizards, rodents, and amphibians.

7. SAN FRANCISCO GARTER SNAKE ....

The San Francisco garter snake lives among vegetation which grows near water. Here, it searches for frogs, toads, small fish, and young mice. It has stripes which come in black, white, a purplish-blue, and vivid red.

8. BOA CONSTRICTOR ....

A boa constrictor will, with perfect timing, seize prey in its mouth, before suffocating the victim by wrapping several coils around its body and squeezing. It is light brown with reddish-brown markings.

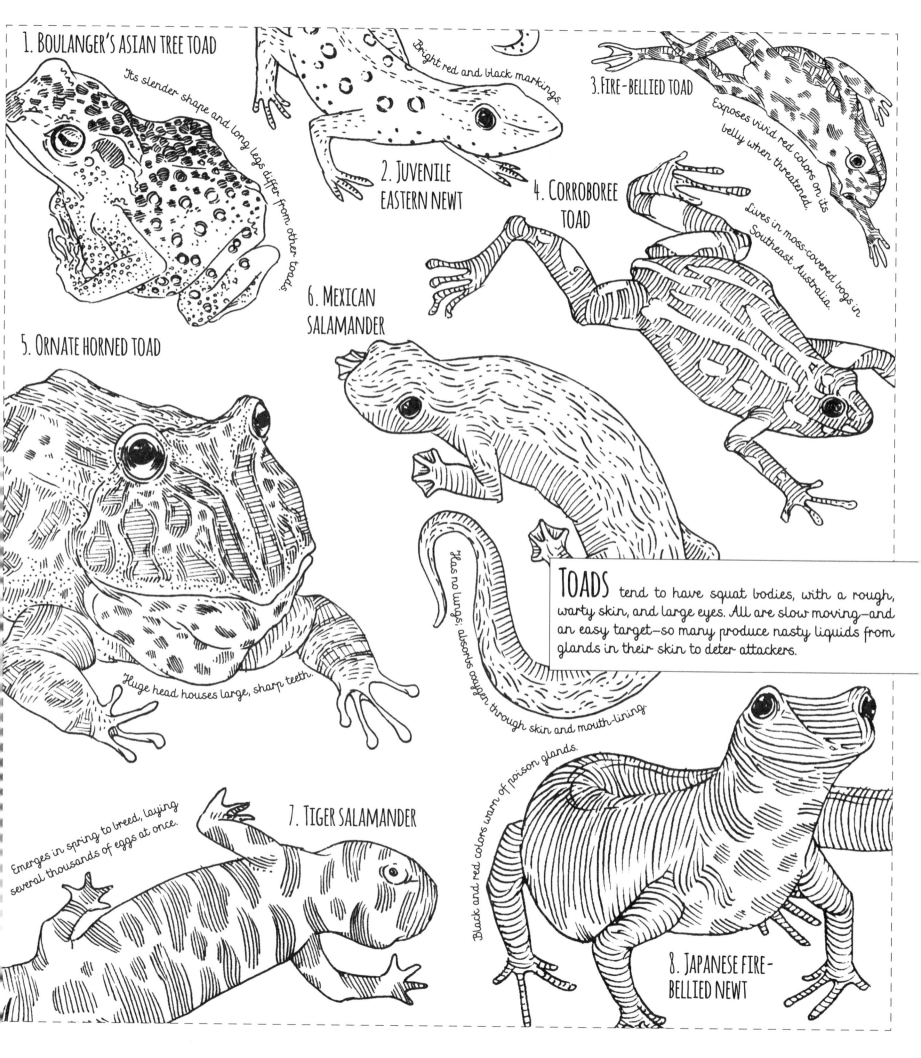

1. BOULANGER'S ASIAN TREE TOAD

Its slender shape and long legs differ from other toads.

Bright red and black markings.

2. JUVENILE EASTERN NEWT

3. FIRE-BELLIED TOAD

Exposes vivid red colors on its belly when threatened.

Lives in moss-covered bogs in Southeast Australia.

4. CORROBOREE TOAD

6. MEXICAN SALAMANDER

5. ORNATE HORNED TOAD

Huge head houses large, sharp teeth.

Has no lungs; absorbs oxygen through skin and mouth-lining.

TOADS tend to have squat bodies, with a rough, warty skin, and large eyes. All are slow moving—and an easy target—so many produce nasty liquids from glands in their skin to deter attackers.

Emerges in spring to breed, laying several thousands of eggs at once.

7. TIGER SALAMANDER

Black and red colors warn of poison glands.

8. JAPANESE FIRE-BELLIED NEWT

Key

1. BOULANGER'S ASIAN TREE TOAD ....

Boulanger's Asian tree toad is unusual; its slender shape and longer legs make it different from other toads. Sticky toe pads are used to climb trees. It is green with yellow spots edged in brown.

2. JUVENILE EASTERN NEWT ....

Bright red, with dark red spots edged in black, the eastern newt warns predators that it is toxic. These newts spend about four years on land in their juvenile form before returning to water to become adults.

3. FIRE-BELLIED TOAD ....

Fire-bellied toads have green backs and very warty skin. When threatened, this species performs the "unken reflex:" it lifts all four limbs over a flattened body, displaying its bright red belly.

4. CORROBOREE TOAD ....

In the more mountainous regions of Southeast Australia, the corroboree toad lives in moss-covered bogs. It is bright yellow with black stripes, but despite this coloring, it is not toxic.

5. ORNATE HORNED TOAD ....

Ornate horned toads have huge heads with a very wide mouth housing large, sharp teeth. Their black and green colors help conceal them as they lie in leaf litter, jumping out to ambush passing prey.

6. MEXICAN SALAMANDER ....

The Mexican mushroom-tongued salamander does not breathe using lungs. Instead, it absorbs oxygen through its skin and mouth lining. It is pink with a black marbling that looks like stripes.

7. TIGER SALAMANDER ....

For most of the year, tiger salamanders live in shallow underground burrows among mosses and leaf litter. In spring, they emerge to breed, laying several thousands of eggs at once. They are green with yellow blotches.

8. JAPANESE FIRE-BELLIED NEWT ....

Black with a red underside and a line of red blotches along its sides, Japanese fire-bellied newts warn predators, through their bright coloring, that they're poisonous.

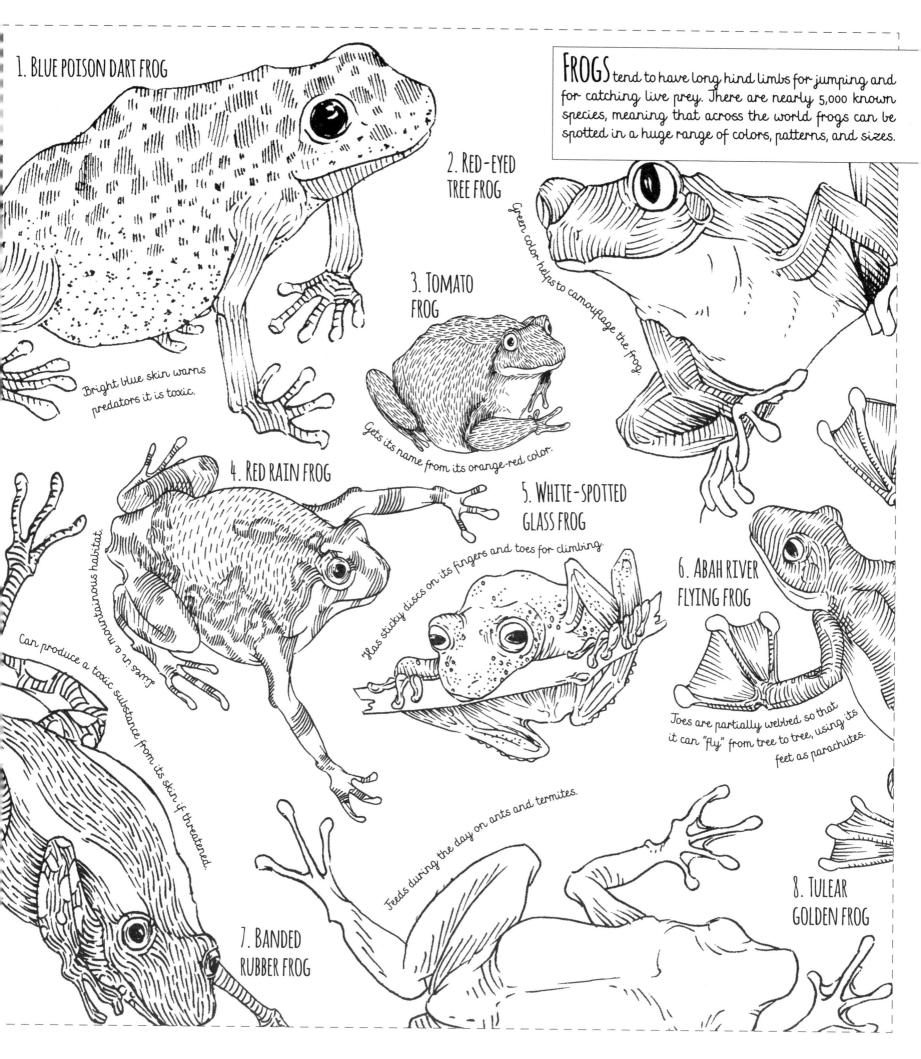

1. BLUE POISON DART FROG

Bright blue skin warns predators it is toxic.

FROGS tend to have long hind limbs for jumping and for catching live prey. There are nearly 5,000 known species, meaning that across the world frogs can be spotted in a huge range of colors, patterns, and sizes.

2. RED-EYED TREE FROG

Green color helps to camouflage the frog.

3. TOMATO FROG

Gets its name from its orange-red color.

4. RED RAIN FROG

Can produce a toxic substance from its skin if threatened.

Lives in a mountainous habitat.

5. WHITE-SPOTTED GLASS FROG

Has sticky discs on its fingers and toes for climbing.

Feeds during the day on ants and termites.

6. ABAH RIVER FLYING FROG

Toes are partially webbed so that it can "fly" from tree to tree, using its feet as parachutes.

7. BANDED RUBBER FROG

8. TULEAR GOLDEN FROG

KEY

1. BLUE POISON DART FROG ....

The bright blue skin of the blue poison dart frog warns predators that it is able to produce a toxic substance if it's attacked. Its spots are dark blue. This frog is active in the daytime.

2. RED-EYED TREE FROG ....

During the day, the red-eyed tree frog rests on leaves with its legs folded, utilizing its green coloring to blend in with the background. When hunting insects, its bright red eyes and blue sides can be seen.

3. TOMATO FROG ....

When the tomato frog is threatened it produces a white, sticky substance on its skin, to repel the attacker. It gets its name from its orange-red color and round shape. Female tomato frogs are larger than males.

4. RED RAIN FROG ....

The Madagascan red rain frog lives on land in a mountainous habitat. When disturbed, it is able to inflate itself. Its back is white with a large red patch, surrounded by bright green and black marbling.

5. WHITE-SPOTTED GLASS FROG ....

White-spotted glass frogs have large, sticky discs on their fingers and toes, making them excellent climbers. Females lay eggs on the underside of leaves. They are very pale green with white spots all over.

6. ABAH RIVER FLYING FROG ....

The Abah river frog's large toes are partially webbed. They can launch themselves from one tree to another, escaping predators by "flying" and using their feet as parachutes. They are bright green with white spots.

7. BANDED RUBBER FROG ....

The banded rubber frog has a fairly plump body and short legs, so it rarely jumps. When threatened, it produces a toxic substance from its skin. It is black with red markings.

8. TULEAR GOLDEN FROG ....

The tulear golden frog has a bright yellow back and head, blue legs and underneath, and black sides. Like poison dart frogs, the bright colors indicate that they are toxic. It feeds during the day, on ants and termites.

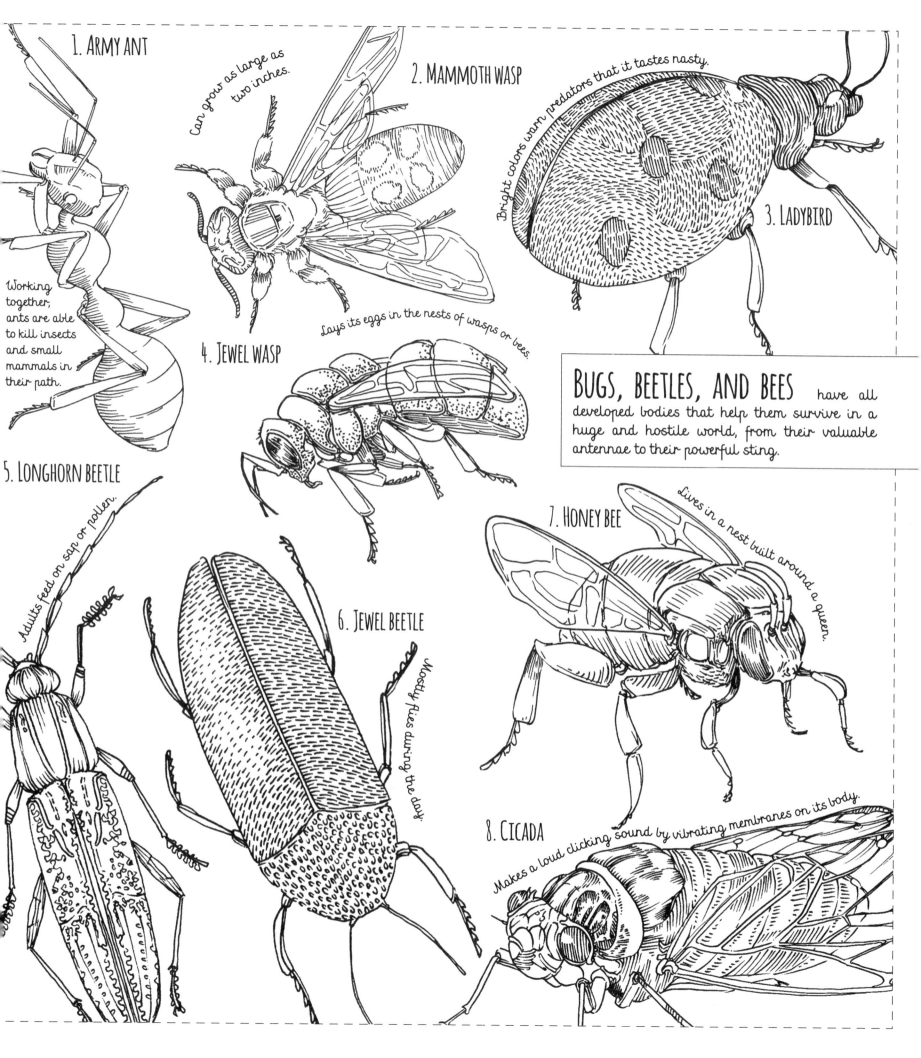

1. ARMY ANT

Can grow as large as two inches.

Working together, ants are able to kill insects and small mammals in their path.

2. MAMMOTH WASP

Bright colors warn predators that it tastes nasty.

3. LADYBIRD

4. JEWEL WASP

Lays its eggs in the nests of wasps or bees.

BUGS, BEETLES, AND BEES have all developed bodies that help them survive in a huge and hostile world, from their valuable antennae to their powerful sting.

5. LONGHORN BEETLE

Adults feed on sap or pollen.

6. JEWEL BEETLE

Mostly flies during the day.

7. HONEY BEE

Lives in a nest built around a queen.

8. CICADA

Makes a loud clicking sound by vibrating membranes on its body.

KEY

1. ARMY ANT

Army ants do not build permanent nests. They move in large groups through tropical forests where they are feared hunters, able to kill insects and even small mammals. They are dark reddish-brown.

2. MAMMOTH WASP

Mammoth wasps can grow as large as two inches. Their heads and bodies are black with red splotches. A female will lay her egg on the larvae of beetles. When the egg hatches, the wasp larva will eat the beetle larvae.

3. LADYBIRD BEETLE

Ladybirds feed on aphids that damage plants. This common species is red with seven black spots, warning predators that it tastes nasty. It can also ooze a foul orange liquid from its leg joints to deter attackers.

4. JEWEL WASP

Female jewel wasps lay an egg in bees' or wasps' nests. The larva hatches and feeds on the host's larvae. To protect it from the stings of bees and other wasps, it has a hard body, which is bright metallic green.

5. LONGHORN BEETLE

Longhorn beetles are a streaky brown color and have elongated antennae. Eggs hatch into larvae which bore into trees, possessing a micro-organism that allows them to digest the wood. Adults feed on sap and pollen.

6. JEWEL BEETLE

With their bright green, often metallic colors, jewel beetles are some of the most attractive insects. Most jewel beetles fly during the day when their colors shine the brightest. Adults feed on nectar and pollen.

7. HONEY BEE

Black and yellow honey bees live in a nest built around a queen who can lay as many as 1,500 eggs a day. Different groups have different tasks, such as collecting nectar and pollen, making honey, feeding, and caring for larvae.

8. CICADA

Cicadas make loud buzzing and clicking sounds by vibrating membranes on their abdomens, using different calls to raise the alarm or attract a mate. They have a black and yellow head and body, and yellow wings.

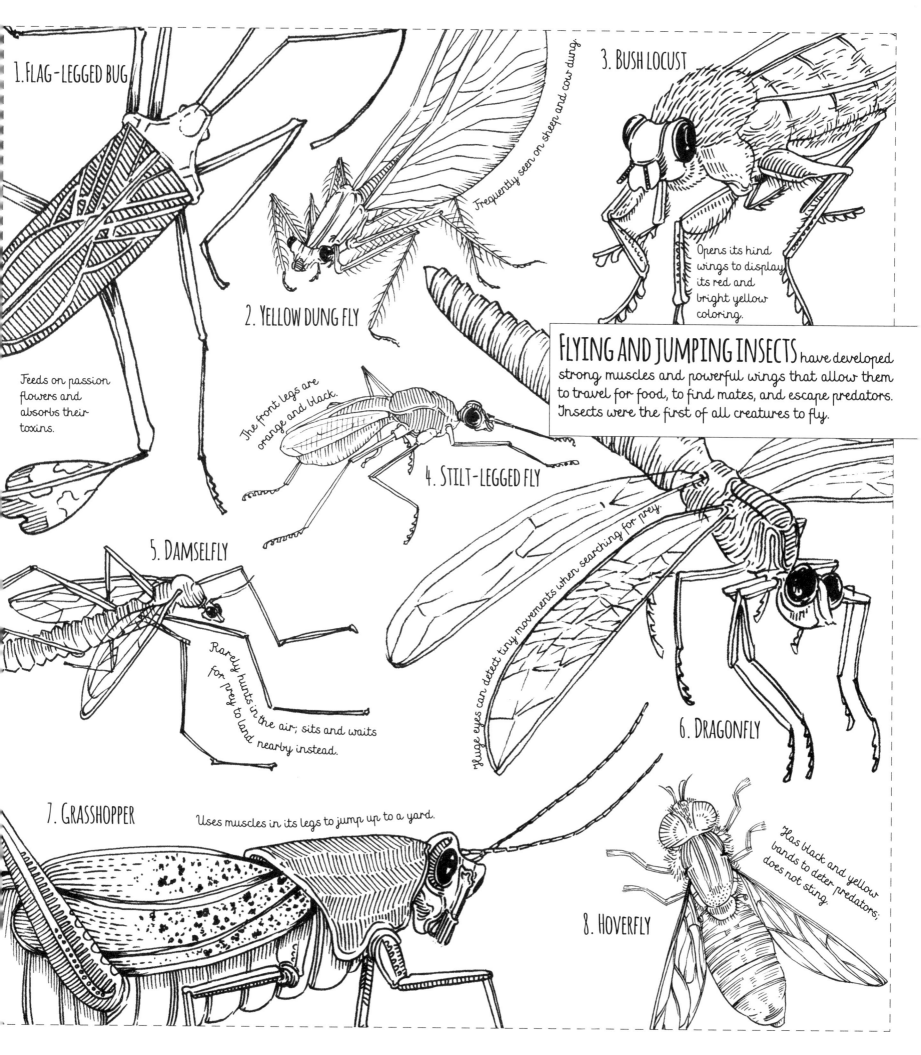

1. FLAG-LEGGED BUG

Feeds on passion flowers and absorbs their toxins.

2. YELLOW DUNG FLY

Frequently seen on sheep and cow dung.

3. BUSH LOCUST

Opens its hind wings to display its red and bright yellow coloring.

FLYING AND JUMPING INSECTS have developed strong muscles and powerful wings that allow them to travel for food, to find mates, and escape predators. Insects were the first of all creatures to fly.

The front legs are orange and black.

4. STILT-LEGGED FLY

5. DAMSELFLY

Rarely hunts in the air; sits and waits for prey to land nearby instead.

Huge eyes can detect tiny movements when searching for prey.

6. DRAGONFLY

7. GRASSHOPPER

Uses muscles in its legs to jump up to a yard.

Has black and yellow bands to deter predators; does not sting.

8. HOVERFLY

Key

1. FLAG-LEGGED BUG ....

Feeding on passion flowers, flag-legged bugs absorb toxins. Their bright colors—orange heads; green bodies, and yellow, red and black legs—act as a warning to predators: Keep away.

2. YELLOW DUNG FLY ....

These dung flies are yellow, with slender, hairy legs, and are frequently seen on sheep and cow dung. They are important because the eggs are laid in dung and the hatching larvae help to break it down to useful manure.

3. BUSH LOCUST ....

Locusts are related to grasshoppers. When jumping away from predators, they open their hind wings, displaying bright yellow and red coloring. They can also produce a foamy toxic fluid.

4. STILT-LEGGED FLY ....

The orange and black front legs of the male stilt-legged fly are used to send out signals to a female. If attracted, she turns her head to "kiss" the mate, while he sits on her back. The head is ruby-colored and the body, orange.

5. DAMSELFLY ....

Damselflies often have metallic-blue bodies and rarely hunt in the air. Instead, they sit and wait for suitable prey to land nearby. Eggs are laid on water plants. Their claws are black or purple-brown.

6. DRAGONFLY ....

The fastest insect fliers, dragonflies have four wings—covered in fine red lines—which move independently, helping them hover and fly in any direction. Their red heads have huge eyes that can detect tiny movements.

7. GRASSHOPPER ....

Although adult grasshoppers have two pairs of wings, they are poor fliers. Instead, they use muscles in their upper and lower legs to jump, up to a yard in a single leap. Grasshoppers are usually yellow or green.

8. HOVERFLY ....

With their slender shape and black and yellow bands, hoverflies are often mistaken for wasps. They do not sting, but their wasp-like coloring deters predators. They hover near flowers, feeding on pollen.

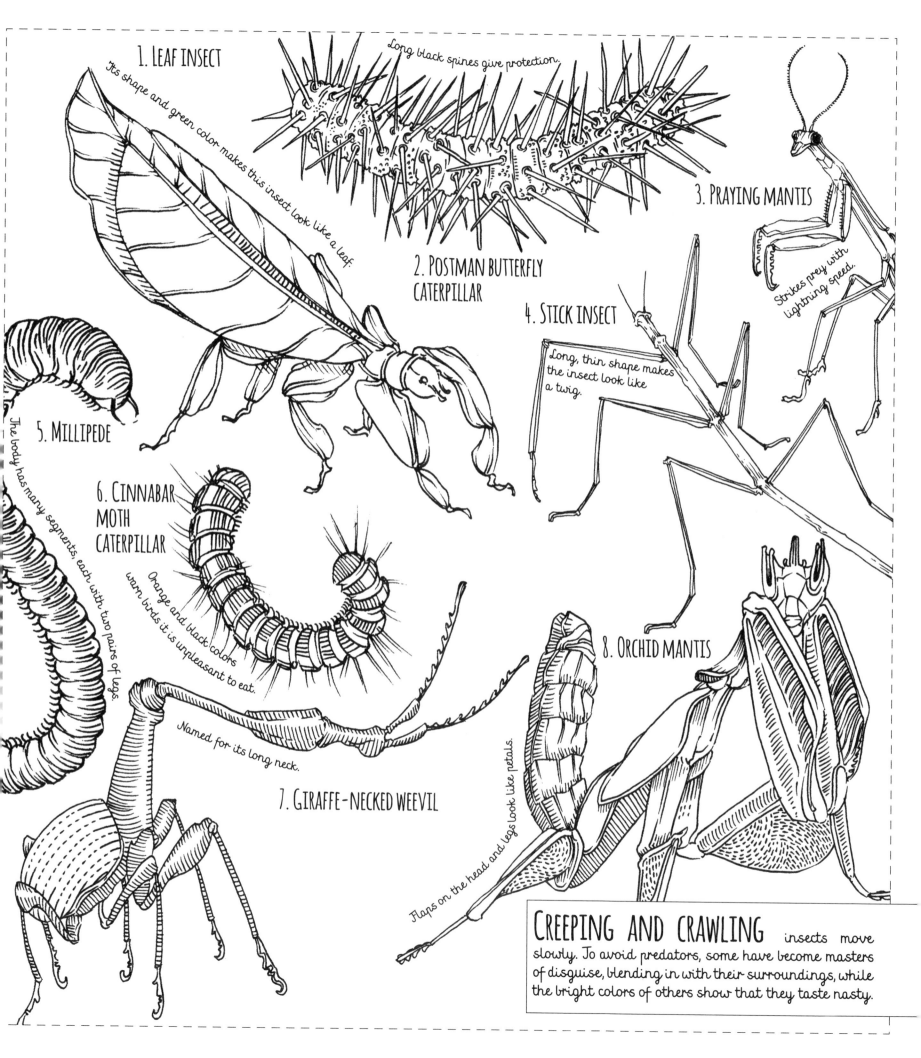

1. LEAF INSECT

Its shape and green color makes this insect look like a leaf.

Long black spines give protection.

3. PRAYING MANTIS

Strikes prey with lightning speed.

2. POSTMAN BUTTERFLY CATERPILLAR

4. STICK INSECT

Long, thin shape makes the insect look like a twig.

5. MILLIPEDE

The body has many segments, each with two pairs of legs.

6. CINNABAR MOTH CATERPILLAR

Orange and black colors warn birds it is unpleasant to eat.

8. ORCHID MANTIS

Named for its long neck.

7. GIRAFFE-NECKED WEEVIL

Flaps on the head and legs look like petals.

CREEPING AND CRAWLING insects move slowly. To avoid predators, some have become masters of disguise, blending in with their surroundings, while the bright colors of others show that they taste nasty.

KEY

1. LEAF INSECT

This insect's green color and leaf-like shape provide perfect camouflage in the rainforest. Its abdomen (middle section) has markings that help disguise this insect even farther.

2. POSTMAN BUTTERFLY CATERPILLAR

Long black spines on the postman butterfly caterpillar give it protection. It has a green and yellow body, and a red head. These colors warn attackers that it contains toxic chemicals, eaten from passion-flower vines.

3. PRAYING MANTIS

Spotting prey first with its enormous eyes, the green praying mantis strikes with lightning speed, holding prey with the spines on the underside of its legs. Its small jaws demand that it nibble the victim's head first.

4. STICK INSECT

A long, thin shape and brown color make the stick insect look like a thin twig, helping it blend in with its surroundings. If attacked, it can repel attackers by squirting unpleasant liquid from glands on its body.

5. MILLIPEDE

Millipedes' bodies are made up of many segments, each with two pairs of legs. The orange-red color of each segment warns it is unpleasant to eat. The millipede roots through leaf litter, chewing on dead leaves.

6. CINNABAR MOTH CATERPILLAR

Cinnabar moths lay their eggs on milkweed, a plant that is dangerous to animals. As the caterpillar feeds, it ingests some of the toxins. Its vivid orange and black colors warn insects and birds that it is nasty to eat.

7. GIRAFFE-NECKED WEEVIL

Giraffe-necked weevils are named for their long necks. Males use them to compete—the one with the longest neck can stay on the leaf where the female is laying her eggs. The head and neck are black and the body red.

8. ORCHID MANTIS

The lilac, green, and white coloring of this mantis matches an orchid. Flaps on the head and legs look like petals. Keeping still protects it from predators and attracts bees, which the mantis catches and eats.

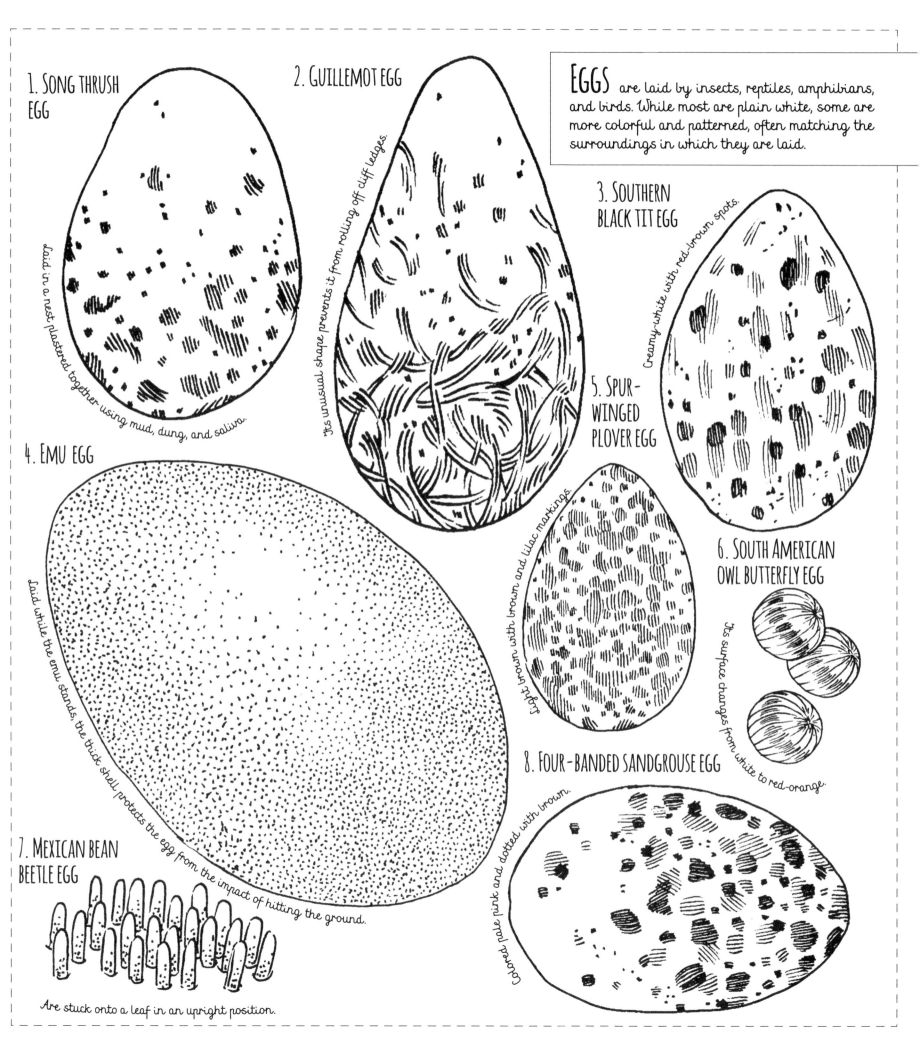

EGGS are laid by insects, reptiles, amphibians, and birds. While most are plain white, some are more colorful and patterned, often matching the surroundings in which they are laid.

1. SONG THRUSH EGG

Laid in a nest plastered together using mud, dung, and saliva.

2. GUILLEMOT EGG

Its unusual shape prevents it from rolling off cliff ledges.

3. SOUTHERN BLACK TIT EGG

Creamy-white with red-brown spots.

4. EMU EGG

Laid while the emu stands, the thick shell protects the egg from the impact of hitting the ground.

5. SPUR-WINGED PLOVER EGG

Light brown with brown and lilac markings.

6. SOUTH AMERICAN OWL BUTTERFLY EGG

Its surface changes from white to red-orange.

7. MEXICAN BEAN BEETLE EGG

Are stuck onto a leaf in an upright position.

8. FOUR-BANDED SANDGROUSE EGG

Colored pale pink and dotted with brown.

KEY

1. Song thrush egg

The song thrush lays its eggs—colored blue with brown spots—in a nest in a tree or in the vines against a wall. The nest is made from twigs, grass, and moss, and is held together using mud, dung, and saliva.

2. Guillemot egg

Guillemots breed on crowded cliffs where ledges for laying eggs are narrow. The unusual shape of the egg prevents it from rolling off. Instead, it rolls around in circles. The eggs are greenish-blue with brown markings.

3. Southern black tit egg

Southern black tits make their nests in tree holes in various parts of Africa. Plant materials are used to soften the base into which three creamy-white eggs with red-brown spots are laid.

4. Emu egg

Emus lay their eggs standing up; the dark turquoise eggs have a thick shell that can withstand the impact of hitting the ground. One egg is laid about every three days in the Australian winter months.

5. Spur-winged plover egg

The female spur-winged plover makes a scrape (shallow nest) in mudflats, and lines it with twigs, pebbles, and grass. When nesting in such an open habitat, it is vital that the eggs blend in, so they don't get eaten.

6. South American owl butterfly egg

When first laid on leaves in the tropical rainforest, the eggs of this owl butterfly are white. They take seven days to hatch. During this period, the surface changes from white through to yellow and—finally—red-orange.

7. Mexican bean beetle egg

The yellow eggs of the Mexican bean beetle are stuck on a leaf in an upright or vertical position. At the top of each egg is a ring of pores that allows air to circulate inside it to reach the developing larva.

8. Four-banded sandgrouse egg

The eggs of the four-banded sandgrouse are pale pink, dotted with brown. They are camouflaged by the fallen leaves of an African plant that the sandgrouse uses to make a shallow nest, called a scrape.

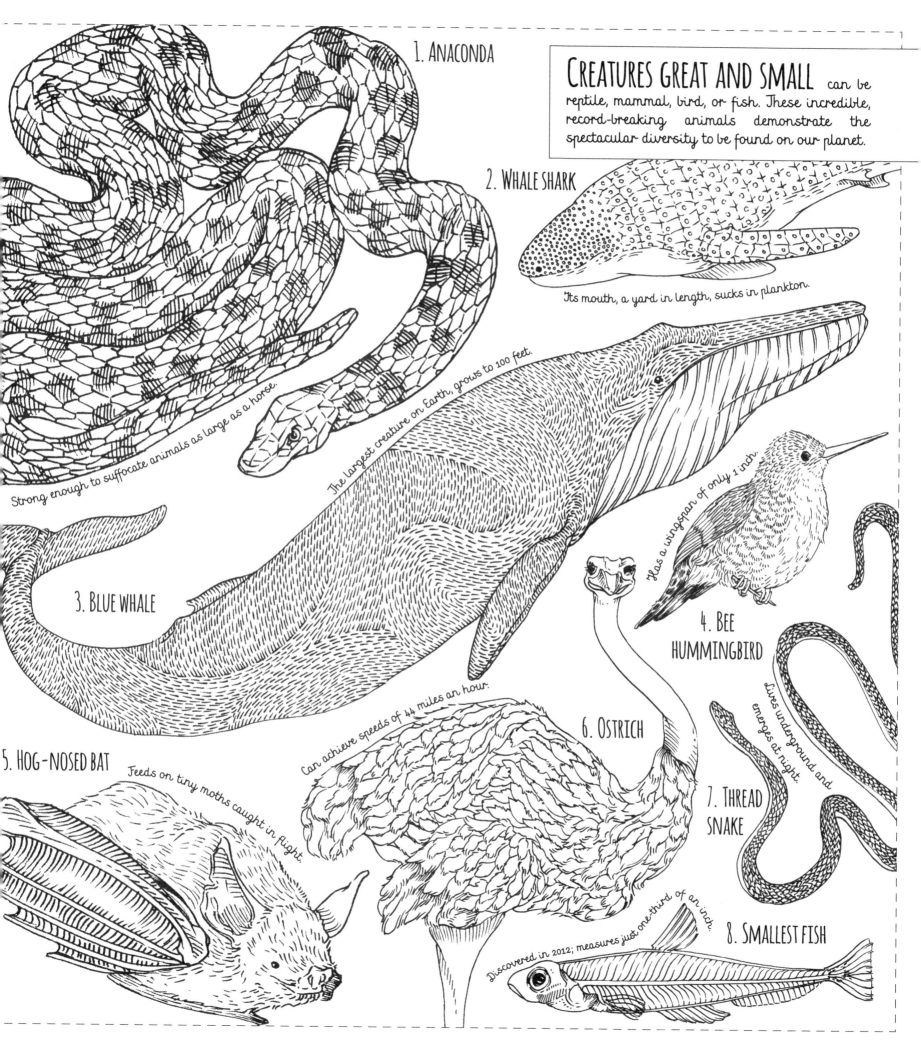

1. ANACONDA

2. WHALE SHARK

Its mouth, a yard in length, sucks in plankton.

Strong enough to suffocate animals as large as a horse.

The largest creature on Earth, grows to 100 feet.

Has a wingspan of only 2 inch.

3. BLUE WHALE

4. BEE HUMMINGBIRD

5. HOG-NOSED BAT

Feeds on tiny moths caught in flight.

Can achieve speeds of 44 miles an hour.

6. OSTRICH

Lives underground and emerges at night.

7. THREAD SNAKE

Discovered in 2012; measures just one-third of an inch.

8. SMALLEST FISH

KEY

1. ANACONDA ....

The 11-yard-long anaconda is strong enough to constrict and suffocate animals as large as a horse. It waits to ambush prey in waterside vegetation, camouflaged by its olive-green color.

2. WHALE SHARK ....

Measuring up to 60 feet, the blueish-green whale shark is the largest fish in the world. While cruising slowly, it opens its yard-wide mouth to suck in huge amounts of plankton-filled water.

3. BLUE WHALE ....

The largest creature on Earth, the blue whale grows to a phenomenal 100 feet long and can eat six tons of food a day, feeding on tiny crustaceans that it filters from the water. It is dark-blue to gray.

4. BEE HUMMINGBIRD ....

With a wingspan of just a single inch, the smallest bird in the world is the bee hummingbird. It has a red head and throat and a green body. Eggs are laid in a cup-shaped nest and are only a quarter-inch long.

5. HOG-NOSED BAT ....

Growing to the size of a bumblebee, the hog-nosed bat is the smallest of all mammals, with a wingspan of less than five inches. This brown bat is found in just a few caves in Thailand and feeds on tiny moths.

6. OSTRICH ....

Long, muscular legs and powerful two-toed feet help the ostrich—the world's largest bird—achieve speeds of 44 miles per hour. It has black feathers with white wings, and a white neck and tail.

7. THREAD SNAKE ....

The thread snake measures about three inches and has a smooth, slender, silvery-pink body. It lives underground, emerging at night. As its eyes are covered with scales, it is hardly able to see.

8. SMALLEST FISH ....

The smallest fish in the world was discovered in 2012. Its pale red body measures just a third of an inch. It has no stomach, using a plate in its skull to help chew food. It hasn't yet been given a name.

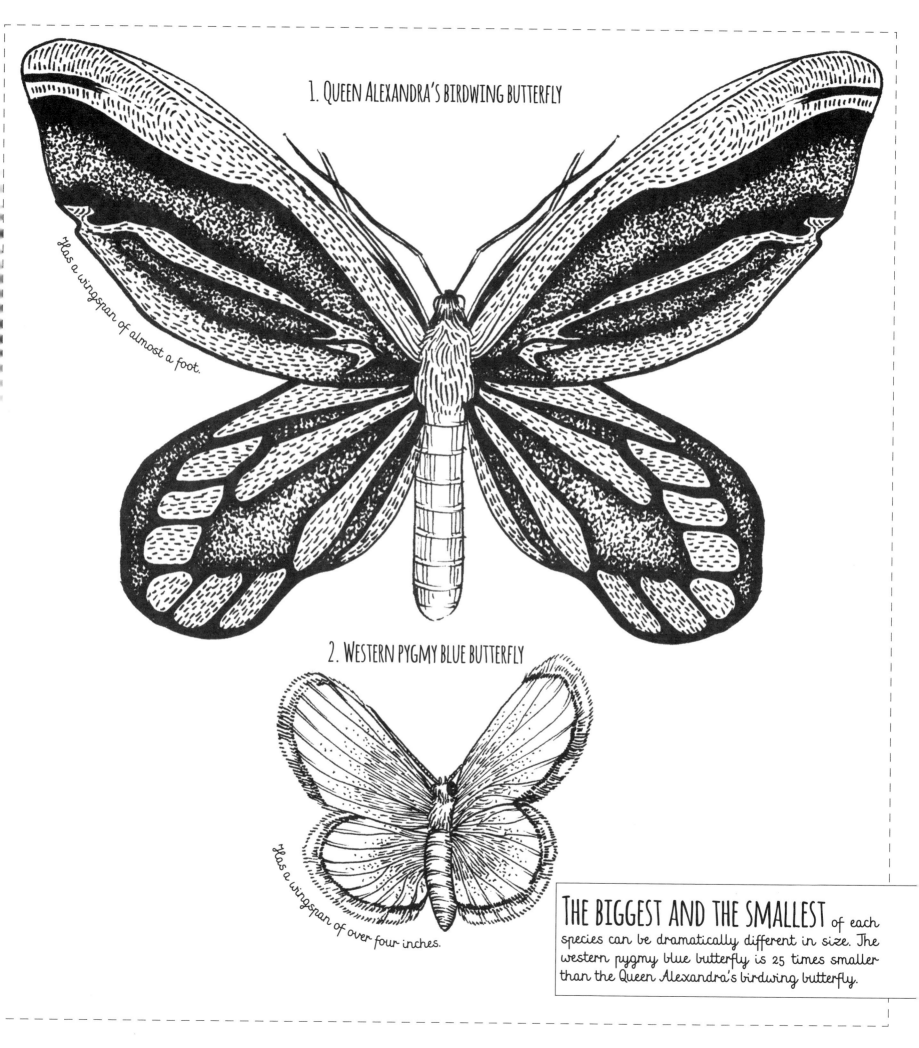

1. QUEEN ALEXANDRA'S BIRDWING BUTTERFLY

Has a wingspan of almost a foot.

2. WESTERN PYGMY BLUE BUTTERFLY

Has a wingspan of over four inches.

THE BIGGEST AND THE SMALLEST of each species can be dramatically different in size. The western pygmy blue butterfly is 25 times smaller than the Queen Alexandra's birdwing butterfly.

1. Queen Alexandra's birdwing butterfly

With a wingspan of nearly a foot, the Queen Alexandra's birdwing butterfly is the largest butterfly in the world. Adults live for about three months, feeding on a single special species of climbing vine. Powerful fliers, they spend early morning and evening feeding high up in the rainforest canopy. Caterpillars are black with red markings and a cream-colored shape. Male butterflies are bright turquoise with a yellow body and a black band across each wing. The Queen Alexandra's birdwing has a unique size and beautiful color, but is also one of the most endangered butterflies in the world.

2. Western pygmy blue butterfly

The western pygmy blue is the world's smallest butterfly. Its wingspan is less than a half-inch, which makes it 25 times smaller than the largest species. Despite its name, the creature has very little actual blue color on its wings. They are grayish-blue near the body but light brown everywhere else. Western pygmy blues are found in the deserts of California, where adults feed on flower nectar. Eggs are laid individually on sage brush plants, which are fed on by emerging caterpillars.